T0340219

Human Capital Development and Indigenous Peoples

In all countries for which data is available, Indigenous peoples have lower rates of formal educational participation and attainment than their non-Indigenous counterparts. There are many structural reasons for this, but it may in part be related to the perceived relationship between the costs and benefits of education. *Human Capital Development and Indigenous Peoples* systematically applies a human capital approach to educational policy, to help understand the education and broader development outcomes of Indigenous peoples.

The basic Human Capital Model states that individuals, families and communities will invest in education until the benefits of doing so no longer outweigh the costs. This trade-off is often considered in monetary terms. Here the author broadens cost-benefit definitions to include health and wellbeing improvements alongside social costs driven by discrimination and unfair treatment in schools. With coverage of the Americas, Asia, Australia and New Zealand, the book critiques existing approaches, and provides an outlet for the self-described experiences of a diverse set of Indigenous peoples on the breadth of educational costs and benefits. Combining new quantitative analysis, cross-national perspectives and an explicit policy focus, this book provides policy actors with a detailed understanding of the education decision and equips them with the knowledge to enhance benefits while minimising costs.

This book will appeal to policy-engaged researchers in the fields of economics, demography, sociology, political science, development studies and anthropology, as well as policy makers or practitioners who are interested in incorporating the most recent evidence into their practice or frameworks.

Nicholas Biddle is Associate Professor in Public Policy at the Australian National University and Associate Director of the ANU Centre for Social Research and Methods. He is also a Senior Fellow at the Centre for Aboriginal Economic Policy Research and a Fellow of the Tax and Transfer Policy Institute.

Routledge Studies in Indigenous Peoples and Policy

There are an estimated 370 million Indigenous Peoples in over 70 countries worldwide, often facing common issues stemming from colonialism and its ongoing effects. Routledge Studies in Indigenous Peoples and Policy brings together books which explore these concerns, including poverty; health inequalities; loss of land, language and culture; environmental degradation and climate change; intergenerational trauma; and the struggle to have their rights, cultures and communities protected.

Indigenous Peoples across the world are asserting their right to fully participate in policy making that affects their people, their communities and the natural world, and to have control over their own communities and lands. This book series explores policy issues, reports on policy research and champions the best examples of methodological approaches. It will explore policy issues from the perspectives of Indigenous Peoples in order to develop evidence-based policy and create policy-making processes that represent Indigenous Peoples and support positive social change.

Human Capital Development and Indigenous Peoples
Nicholas Biddle

Human Capital Development and Indigenous Peoples

Nicholas Biddle

Routledge
Taylor & Francis Group

LONDON AND NEW YORK

First published 2019 by Routledge

2 Park Square, Milton Park, Abingdon, Oxfordshire OX14 4RN

52 Vanderbilt Avenue, New York, NY 10017

Routledge is an imprint of the Taylor & Francis Group, an informa business

First issued in paperback 2020

British Library Cataloguing-in-Publication Data
A catalogue record for this book is available from the British Library

Library of Congress Cataloging-in-Publication Data
A catalog record has been requested for this book

ISBN: 978-1-138-49836-5 (hbk)
ISBN: 978-0-367-50384-0 (pbk)

Typeset in Times New Roman
by Out of House Publishing

Contents

Figures

Preface
Standpoint and position

About the topic

The more we learn about other species, the less unique us *Homo sapiens* seem. Many of the things that we had thought we do well that other animals can't – complex language, creation of tools, co-operation, running for really long distances (Pickering and Bunn 2007) – have been shown to be present in various birds, mammals or even insects to a much greater degree than previously assumed. It may be true that there is no single animal that does all of these things as well as humans, but that is hardly a ringing endorsement.

Martin Seligman and colleagues (2016) have instead argued that the 'unrivaled human ability to be guided by imagining alternatives stretching into the future – "prospection" – uniquely describes *Homo Sapiens.*' We can imagine for ourselves (or for those we care about) a range of future lives, weigh up the pluses and minuses of living these lives, reflect on what it would take to achieve them and make decisions accordingly.

This prospection may be mundane and in the very short term. If I decide to walk to work rather than drive, will the extra exercise and fresh air I get, as well as the amount of money I save on parking, out-weigh the prospect of getting rained on and being in the office a bit later. Even making such a small decision requires me to imagine a healthier, happier me with slightly more money in my bank account, as opposed to a slightly poorer, but drier and more productive version of myself.

This specific decision is only really made on a frequent basis by someone in a very privileged position – someone in a high paying job, in one of the wealthiest and pleasant cities in one of the wealthiest countries in human history. What a person can feasibly imagine and plan for is very context and person specific. But, such prospection is required for the close to infinite number of decisions that humans have been making since they separated from their ancestors.

It is true that many of the decisions that we make do not end up leading to (*ex post*) the best outcome for our future selves. It is often very hard to balance and weight probabilities, and to balance and weight risks (Johnson and Busemeyer 2010). Often, we economise on cognitive load and make decisions rapidly using heuristics or what we might colloquially refer to as 'gut instinct' – the System 1 (fast, instinctive and emotional) thinking that Kahneman (2011) juxtaposes with the deliberative and logical System 2 thinking. We make many of our decisions out of habit, or because that is what we have done the last dozen, or hundred times (Duhigg 2013).

Whatever the imperfections in our decision-making processes, there is increasing evidence that humans are unique in the way they can consider future outcomes and plan accordingly, and importantly that this ability is held across history, across cultures and across domains of decision making.

One of these domains, education, is in many ways the quintessential expression of human prospection. For our very young children, we imagine what their life now and into the future will be like if we enrol them in a particular preschool (perhaps one that is play-based) and compare that with an alternative life if they are enrolled in an alternative preschool (one that focuses on literacy development in a more structured way) or in no preschool at all.

As we reach young adulthood ourselves, we imagine what a given day might be like if we go to school and compare that with the short- and long-term costs and benefits of staying at home, or hanging out with friends at a beach or the mall. When we come to the end of high school, we imagine what our life will be like as a doctor, lawyer, teacher, carpenter, or stay at home parent, and decide whether or not to engage in further training based on how appealing those lives appear and the costs to achieve them.

The Human Capital Model (HCM) is a powerful and intuitive way to conceptualise such education decisions. At its simplest, the HCM states that individuals or their families/community will invest in education until the benefits of doing so no longer outweigh the costs. Often, these benefits and costs are thought of in monetary terms. But this need not be the case. Where richness and complexity can be added to the model is by thinking very carefully about what the range of benefits and costs might be, how they vary across populations and the complicated ways in which they are combined to make an overall decision.

Income is important, but a broader set of benefits might include status within the community; ability to advocate on behalf of one's family and community; health and wellbeing improvements; and intergenerational effects. Economic costs are also important, including the opportunity costs while studying. However, for many people there are social costs of engaging in education, especially if it increases exposure to discrimination and unfair treatment.

And we can have a more expansive definition of what we mean by education. Formal education in a school, university, or early learning setting is one aspect. But so too is learning about one's own language, culture, or country.

This second type of education is particularly important for Indigenous peoples. In almost all countries for which data is available, Indigenous peoples have lower rates of formal education participation and attainment than their non-Indigenous counterparts. There is no evidence or plausible theory to suggest that this is due to lower aptitude (Reich 2018). Rather the benefits of investing in formal education would appear to be less likely to be perceived to outweigh the costs. On the other hand, many Indigenous peoples receive an education about their own land, language and culture that is much richer and deeper than their non-Indigenous counterparts.

The costs and benefits of education, and the type of education options, need therefore to be broadly defined. The ongoing effect of colonisation and the negative view that many Indigenous peoples have of mainstream institutions (based on past negative experiences) impose ongoing social costs. The benefits of education are likely to be reduced if Indigenous peoples experience ongoing discrimination and negative treatment within social and political institutions, as well as in the labour market.

Given the desire of many policy actors (governments, researchers and community leaders) to improve the level of education for Indigenous peoples, it is important to have a detailed understanding of the costs and benefits of education and how they relate to each other. This will help these actors to enhance and highlight the benefits, while minimising costs or reducing barriers.

About the author

It is important to be very clear up front that this book is written by a non-Indigenous researcher, living and working in a particular city, in a particular country, at a particular point in time. I grew up on Darug country,[1] in what is now generally referred to as Western Sydney (Richmond, to be precise). At the time I went to school (from 1984 to 1996), there was very little taught about Indigenous history, culture or peoples.

My mother and father (high school teachers who grew up on Eora and Gumbainggir country, respectively) had even less exposure to Indigenous history or culture than I did. Despite growing up in two households (my parents separated when I was 10) that discussed policy, moral and historical debates quite openly and extensively, there was very little engagement with Indigenous issues either in my local area, or for Australia as a whole.

In 2000, while undertaking an Honours year in Economics at the University of Sydney, I wrote a thesis on the factors associated with the underemployment of Aboriginal and Torres Strait Islander Australians. The topic for my thesis was motivated mainly by the desire to understand the consequences of the education decision and its consequences for development. I had originally wanted to gain this understanding in a developing country context, but with limited time and funds, made the decision to focus on a population group and context for which I could reasonably easily access data. The 1994 National Aboriginal and Torres Strait Islander Survey (NATSIS) was a relatively under-utilised dataset at that point in time, and I ended up undertaking some descriptive and econometric analysis, focusing on the relationship between an Indigenous adult's education levels and their outcomes in the labour market.

The resultant thesis hardly set the academic world alight. However, in writing and researching the paper, my interest in the economic outcomes of Aboriginal and Torres Strait Islander Australians in particular, and Indigenous peoples the world over in general, was sparked. The year 2000 was also a time of reflection and debate in Australia on our national identity and history. The Sydney Olympics took place in September of that year (a distraction for someone trying to write an Honours thesis I might add) with Cathy Freeman[2] providing iconic images as she lit the Olympic flame and then ten days later won gold in the 400 metre sprint, carrying both the Australian and the Aboriginal flag on her victory lap.

In addition to the Olympics, many Australians will still remember taking part in or seeing the images of the Walk for Reconciliation across Sydney Harbour Bridge, on the 28th of May of that year. According to the National Museum of Australia,[3] 'The Bridge Walk for Reconciliation and similar events that took place around Australia in the weeks following were collectively the biggest demonstration of public support for a cause that has ever taken place in Australia' and 'The march was a public expression of support for meaningful reconciliation between Australia's Indigenous and non-Indigenous peoples.'

In 2001, I moved to the Australian capital, Canberra, a city planned by the newly formed Commonwealth of Australia in 1913, built on the lands of the Ngunnawal people. I started full-time work at the Australian Bureau of Statistics (ABS) that year, working on inequality, health, wellbeing and poverty measurement/analysis.

In late 2003 I commenced a PhD at the Centre for Aboriginal Economic Policy Research (CAEPR), at the Australian National University. I would eventually write a thesis titled 'Does it pay to go to school? The benefits of and participation in education of Indigenous Australians' and graduate in late 2007, drawing on a range of quantitative datasets to further understand the education decision of Indigenous Australians.

After a brief return to the ABS, I then commenced full-time work at CAEPR, extending my research to broader economic, demographic and social issues related to the Aboriginal and Torres Strait Islander population. I now work at the ANU Centre for Social Research and Methods, focusing on evaluating and analysing policy for its impact on the lives of the Australian population, and those in the Asia-Pacific region.

This short history is not written to demonstrate particular expertise or insights; although I have learnt a fair bit along the way about how we can best use, but also critique data about particular populations. Rather, it is written under the principle that a person's history, experiences and background shape the type of research that they do, the types of questions they ask and the conclusions they draw from that research. Indigenous researchers in Australia and all over the world are critiquing research that intentionally or otherwise privileges non-Indigenous frameworks and epistemologies (Foley 2006). Indigenous researchers are becoming increasingly prominent in academic debates, telling their stories, answering their questions and driving policy change (albeit much slower than many would like).

As a non-Indigenous author, I could never speak for Indigenous peoples in Australia, let alone elsewhere. It would be foolish and dangerous to identify policy priorities or claim insider knowledge. But, and this is a little more controversial, that doesn't mean that non-Indigenous authors can't write about data and evidence related to Indigenous peoples. This must be done though carefully and with humility.

As someone who has lived and travelled to many Indigenous nations across Australia, urban, regional and remote, I have experienced contemporary Indigenous culture as an outsider and someone in a position of power and prestige (to the extent that academics still have power and prestige). I have travelled to other countries and met Indigenous peoples from Asia, the Pacific, the Americas and the circumpolar north, visiting their lands briefly and learning more each time about what I do not know. I have lectured to, supervised and co-authored with a number of

Indigenous scholars, who in almost all cases have taught me more than I have taught them.

This experience and history has shaped my worldview and the questions that I seek answers to. It has made me aware of the need to privilege Indigenous perspectives when writing and speaking about Indigenous issues. It has shown to me the absolute imperative to recognise diversity within Indigenous populations in terms of priorities, aspirations and perspectives, across the dimensions of gender, geography, generations and, although it can be seen as a dirty word in Australia, class. But it has also made me aware of the shared worldview of many Indigenous peoples across all continents around the importance of land, language and culture for a genuinely prosperous past, present and future.

Finally, this experience has taught me to respect the genuine agency of Indigenous peoples in shaping future policy priorities and settings. At the same time though, there is often too little focus on non-Indigenous peoples as policy targets and contributors to improved outcomes for Indigenous peoples whether as teachers, employers, colleagues, peers or voters.

Walter (2016) argues that research on 'Indigenous statistics' focuses on five D's: 'disparity, deprivation, disadvantage, dysfunction and difference' and that this creates a misleading picture of Indigenous circumstance. The methodology employed within this book attempts to avoid these '5 D's' by highlighting that in certain cases Indigenous children and youth have better outcomes than otherwise comparable non-Indigenous counterparts, that observable characteristics that correlate with but don't define Indigeneity often explain much or all of the difference between the two populations, and that a policy approach that attempts to identify the structural barriers to education participation rather than emphasising deficiencies within Indigenous children and youth themselves are likely to be more effective, and arguably have much greater support.

About the book

The aim of this book is therefore to utilise the HCM to help understand the development options and constraints for Indigenous peoples internationally; summarise and critique existing policy approaches to improve the education experience of Indigenous peoples; and provide an outlet for the views and experiences of a diverse set of Indigenous peoples on what the breadth of costs and benefits of education might be.

New analysis will be presented, based mainly on secondary analysis of existing datasets, and focusing on Australia and the US, where data is most accessible. This analysis will have been undertaken by a non-Indigenous researcher, but draw on data that has had considerable input from Indigenous peoples.

It will draw heavily upon research in an Australian context, but also draw on data and lessons from other countries and contexts (particularly the Canadian, New Zealand and American experience). Finally, it will reflect on implications for policy and practice. Policy goals and priorities should be, and increasingly are being shaped by Indigenous peoples. However, it is up to a much wider community to contribute information and effort to make the achievement of those goals and priorities much more of a reality.

Notes

1 https://aiatsis.gov.au/explore/articles/aiatsis-map-indigenous-australia.
2 https://aiatsis.gov.au/explore/articles/cathy-freeman.
3 www.nma.gov.au/online_features/defining_moments/featured/walk-for-reconciliation.

References

Duhigg, C. (2013). *The power of habit: Why we do what we do and how to change*, London: Random House.
Foley, D. (2006). "Indigenous standpoint theory." *International Journal of the Humanities* **3**(8): 25–36.
Johnson, J. G. and J. R. Busemeyer (2010). "Decision making under risk and uncertainty." *Wiley Interdisciplinary Reviews: Cognitive Science* **1**(5): 736–749.
Kahneman, D. (2011). *Thinking, fast and slow*, London: Penguin Books.
Pickering, T. R. and H. T. Bunn (2007). "The endurance running hypothesis and hunting and scavenging in savanna-woodlands." *Journal of Human Evolution* **53**(4): 434–438.
Reich, D. (2018). *Who we are and how we got here: Ancient DNA and the new science of the human past*, Oxford, UK: Oxford University Press.
Seligman, M. E., P. Railton, R. F. Baumeister and C. Sripada (2016). *Homo prospectus*, Oxford, UK: Oxford University Press.
Walter, M. (2016). Data politics and Indigenous representation in Australian statistics. *Indigenous Data Sovereignty: Toward an Agenda,* J. Taylor and T. Kukutai (eds). Canberra: ANU Press.

Part I

A human capital approach to Indigenous development

1   Introduction

Why human capital, and why Indigenous peoples?

How we start a journey shapes, if not determines, whether and how we reach our destination. And so it is important to take care with definitions and concepts that we will use in the remainder of this book. I begin with a discussion of how we define Indigenous peoples, how the Human Capital Model has been conceptualised and characterised, and then discuss different ways to measure development.

Who is Indigenous?

There are very few people through history who have had demonstrable impact on domestic policy, international law and the academy. One of these, Emeritus Professor Mick Dodson, is a member of the Yawuru peoples, traditional owners of land and waters in the Broome area of the southern Kimberley region of Western Australia, former Director of the National Centre for Indigenous Studies at the ANU and the 2009 Australian of the Year. He also contributed to the drafting of the text of the Declaration of the Rights of Indigenous Peoples and wrote about his experience as follows (Dodson 1998):

> My first session at the UN Working Group on Indigenous Populations was a moment of tremendous insight and recognition. I was sitting in a room, 12,000 miles away from home [in New York], but if I had closed my eyes I could just about have been in Maningrida or Doomadgee or Flinders Island. The people wore different clothes, spoke in different languages or with different accents, and their homes had different names. But the stories and the sufferings were the same. We were all part of a world community of Indigenous peoples spanning the planet; experiencing the same problems and struggling against the same alienation, marginalisation and sense of powerlessness. We had gathered there united

by our shared frustration with the dominant systems in our own countries and their consistent failure to deliver justice. We were all looking for, and demanding, justice from a higher authority.

As Professor Dodson describes it, the people in that room came from six different continents, but all had a shared identity as Indigenous peoples. They may not have needed a statistical definition to know that they shared that identity, but most would have been keenly aware of the way in which such definitions have sometimes helped, but often hurt their compatriots.

In (1987), Jose Martinez Cobo, the then Special Rapporteur of the UN Sub-Commission on Prevention of Discrimination and Protection of Minorities gave this definition:

> Indigenous communities, peoples and nations are those which, having a historical continuity with pre-invasion and pre-colonial societies that developed on their territories, consider themselves distinct from other sectors of the societies now prevailing on those territories, or parts of them. They form at present non-dominant sectors of society and are determined to preserve, develop and transmit to future generations their ancestral territories, and their ethnic identity, as the basis of their continued existence as peoples, in accordance with their own cultural patterns, social institutions and legal system.

Countries and peoples have operationalised this and similar definitions in very different ways across time and across space (Kukutai 2004; Kukutai and Taylor 2013; Kukutai and Walter 2015; Liebler 2018). Some have used tribal registries, many of which include complicated rules for inclusion or exclusion that are influenced by gender and marital norms (Haozous, Strickland et al. 2014). Other countries or systems are based on the use of Indigenous languages (usually as opposed to English, Spanish, French or Portuguese) as a measure of Indigenous status. A limited number of countries (in particular the US and Brazil) explicitly ask about a person's race, although it should be mentioned that this was the method for a greater number of countries historically. Finally, a growing number of countries and Indigenous communities use self-identification for determining whether someone is Indigenous, albeit often with a requirement for some form of community acceptance. Using this mix of definitions, a recent estimate places the global Indigenous population at around 370 million people (Hall and Patrinos 2012), though this is likely to be a significant under-estimate.

None of the above methods of identification is value neutral, and none avoids the problem of missing people who would otherwise be identified using a different approach. More controversially, they all have the potential to include people as Indigenous who might not be accepted as such by others in the community (Indigenous or otherwise).

In Australia where I live and work, the official approach is to take a tri-partite definition. Specifically, a person is typically classified as Indigenous if:

- they are of Aboriginal or Torres Strait Islander descent;
- they identify as an Aboriginal or Torres Strait Islander; and
- they are accepted as an Aboriginal or a Torres Strait Islander by the community in which they live.

In practice, many of the Indigenous people who are the focus of policy in Australia come from a single question on the (five-yearly) Census of Population and Housing. This question is not asked of each individual, but rather is usually filled in by a representative member of the household as follows (from the 2016 Census): 'Is the person of Aboriginal or Torres Strait Islander origin?'

By way of comparison, in New Zealand/Aotearoa, a much richer level set of questions are asked, with individuals who fill in the 2018 Census separately asked for their ethnicity, their Māori descent, the name of their Iwi (roughly translated as tribe) and their language spoken. An even bigger difference between the way in which Indigenous status is incorporated in the Australian and New Zealand context is the relative ease which with those in New Zealand are able to access and complete a Census form in Māori language.

Whatever the method, those who use or make decisions based on such official statistics need to be aware that Indigenous identity and identification is in part a social construct, which individuals and communities accept or reject in different ways at different points in time. Furthermore, Indigenous identification tends to be increasing, particularly in the English-speaking settler-colonial states of Australia, Canada, New Zealand and the United States (Kukutai and Webber 2017; Markham and Biddle 2017; Liebler 2018). There is also evidence, however, that Indigenous populations are growing in less developed parts of the world (McSweeney and Arps 2005; Sirén 2007), though this growth is less consistent and more difficult to measure than in more developed parts of the world.

In part, this growth is driven by natural population increase – an excess of births over deaths – partly driven by increasing rates of mixed partnering between Indigenous and non-Indigenous adults (and the children of those partnerships being identified as Indigenous (Kukutai 2007)). However, there is also very strong evidence that population growth is being driven by an increasing propensity for people with Indigenous ancestry to identify as such in official collections, even with relatively consistent data collection practices (Guimond 1999; Malenfant, Coulombe et al. 2012, Markham and Biddle 2018).

What is human capital?

The Human Capital Model, or HCM, in more or less its current form was outlined by Becker (1964) and then revised in Becker (1994). At the heart of the model is the assumption that when deciding whether or not to undertake a certain type of education, potential students are rational (in the economic sense) utility maximisers who, above all, see education as an investment. An investment in education will improve one's performance in the workplace and an individual will invest until the returns to an additional unit of education (measured by increases in discounted future income) just equal the cost. That is, until marginal returns equal marginal cost. According to Becker (1994),

> Schooling, a computer training course, expenditures on medical care, and lectures on the virtues of punctuality and honesty are capital too in the sense that they improve health, raise earnings, or add to a person's appreciation of literature over much of his or her lifetime.

This traditional definition of human capital is very European-centric (for example the reference to literature as opposed to other forms of cultural expression). However it need not be interpreted in such a way. A broader definition of human capital would be the 'knowledge, skills, competencies and attributes that allow people to contribute to their personal and social well-being, as well as that of their countries', or more succinctly, a person's 'skills, learning, talents, and attributes' (Keeley 2007).

What is development?

The HCM is a theory, or a way of viewing and explaining the decisions that individuals and families make when engaging with different forms of education and health decisions. The validity of that theory is based almost exclusively on the extent to which it explains or predicts the decisions that we observe people actually making. The concept of development that one uses, on the other hand, has the potential to directly influence policy and practice.

The United Nations Declaration on the Rights of Indigenous Peoples (UNDRIP) makes clear that the concept of development used to guide policy development for and with Indigenous peoples should be based firmly on the needs and aspirations of that population. Four articles, in particular, deal with this explicitly:

- Article 3 – Indigenous peoples have the right of self-determination. By virtue of that right they freely determine their political status and freely pursue their economic, social and cultural development.
- Article 21 (1) – Indigenous peoples have the right, without discrimination, to the improvement of their economic and social conditions, including, inter alia, in the areas of education, employment, vocational training and retraining, housing, sanitation, health and social security.
- Article 23 – Indigenous peoples have the right to determine and develop priorities and strategies for exercising their right to development. In particular, Indigenous peoples have the right to be actively involved in developing and determining health, housing and other economic and social programmes affecting them and, as far as possible, to administer such programmes through their own institutions.
- Article 32 (1) – Indigenous peoples have the right to determine and develop priorities and strategies for the development or use of their lands or territories and other resources.

Different states have operationalised these (and related) articles to different degrees. In Australia, the main policy focus has been on specific policy targets that generally take the outcomes of the non-Indigenous population as a benchmark and compare the gap between the two populations and whether it is changing over time. The specific Closing the Gap targets are:[1]

- close the gap in life expectancy within a generation (by 2031);
- halve the gap in mortality rates for Indigenous children under 5 within a decade (by 2018);
- 95 per cent of all Indigenous 4-year-olds enrolled in early childhood education (by 2025) – renewed target;
- close the gap between Indigenous and non-Indigenous school attendance within five years (by 2018);

- halve the gap for Indigenous children in reading, writing and numeracy achievements within a decade (by 2018);
- halve the gap in Year 12 attainment (or equivalent attainment rates) for Indigenous Australians aged 20–24 (by 2020);
- halve the gap in employment outcomes between Indigenous and non-Indigenous Australians within a decade (by 2018).

The headline target (closing the life expectancy gap) was one that was driven by Indigenous peoples in Australia (and particularly, the 2004–2010 Aboriginal and Torres Strait Islander Social Justice Commissioner, Tom Calma (2010)) and arguably sits well within the UNDRIP. However, the overall agenda has been criticised as not taking into account Indigenous-specific needs and aspirations, for being overly focused on non-Indigenous norms and of not having adequately involved Indigenous peoples in the implementation and measurement (Altman 2009).

One concept of development that has the flexibility to incorporate Indigenous notions is the capability approach, first developed by Amartya Sen (2001) who argues that policy should focus on capabilities or what 'people are able to do or able to be – the opportunity they have to achieve various lifestyles and as a result, the ability to live a good life.' This, however, is in direct comparison (in his terminology) to functionings or the things that a person actually does or experiences. Sen (2004) argues that there are two kinds of human functioning: elementary ones such as being in good health, nourished, sheltered and the more complex, social ones such as having self-respect and taking part in the life of the community. He argues that the conversion of capabilities into functioning is influenced by individual, family and community factors and values; and the environment in which they live.

One of the leading proponents of the capabilities approach in Indigenous affairs is Noel Pearson and the Cape York Institute (CYI). In articulating their approach, the CYI states that their main goal can 'be expressed as ensuring that Cape York people have the capabilities to choose a life they value. It is not about making choices for people, but is rather about expanding the range of choices people have available to them' (Pearson 2005).

There is substantial overlap between the capability measures in Nussbaum (2000) and Pearson (2005). Where the former lists 'having the right to seek employment on an equal basis with others' as an aspect of the control over one's environment, the latter lists 'the number and type of employment opportunities for members of the community' as the first – and one might assume most important – capability.

Furthermore, whereas the CYI lists 'the ability to access a quality education' as a key capability, Nussbaum (2000) outlines the goal of being 'informed and cultivated by an adequate education, including, but by no means limited to, literacy and basic mathematical and scientific training'.

Some of the capabilities listed by the CYI could perhaps be better thought of as functionings though. For example, although a person's income does impact on their consumption possibilities, income is in many contexts an outcome of the choices that one makes, rather than a measure of the economic resources that are potentially available to an individual. For example, a person who opts out of the labour market in order to have or raise children (or to engage in other non-market activities) has the same capabilities as one who continues to work, despite having a lower level of income. The same could be said of net worth of a household or individual which will be influenced by the choices that individuals have made over their lifecourse.

Finally, the use of income passivity as a measure of negative capabilities is potentially problematic. There are many individuals, for example those with a disability or those who are unable to obtain employment despite their best efforts, for whom unearned income is the only way in which they are able to meet their other capabilities of adequate housing, quality health services or consumption.

Other countries, or other Indigenous communities, have focused more heavily on Indigenous-specific notions of wellbeing as the drivers of development approaches. This has been particularly prominent in Aotearoa/New Zealand where Te Whāiti, McCarthy et al. (1997) have stated that they 'believe that health development is an on-going process that requires the delicate balancing of a number of factors that are both internal and external to individuals and whānau' (roughly, but incompletely translated as family). In later writing, Durie (2006) stated that:

> The measurement of Māori wellbeing requires an approach that is able to reflect Māori world views, especially the close relationship between people and the environment. This ecological orientation carries with it an expectation that social, economic and environmental aspects of wellbeing will be given adequate consideration and that cultural and physical resources will be similarly considered alongside personal wellbeing. In short there is no single measure of wellbeing; instead a range of measures are necessary so that the circumstances of individuals and groups, as well as the relationships, perspectives, and assets within te ao Māori can be quantified and monitored.

More recently, Yap and Yu (2016) attempted to 'operationalise the capability approach' by incorporating Indigenous worldviews. The authors used a participatory approach and argued that 'utilisation of the capability approach here provides an opportunity not only to understand conceptualisations of wellbeing but also to sketch the pathways towards achieving wellbeing.' Their approach identified a number of indicators of wellbeing that are held commonly between Indigenous and non-Indigenous Australians (for example housing, income and health), as well as others that were more Indigenous specific (for example cultural events, Yawuru language, and law and ceremonies).

The aim of this chapter or this book is not to revisit the complexity and depth of research around Indigenous notions of wellbeing. Indeed, I have discussed this in some depth using data from the National Aboriginal and Torres Strait Islander Social Survey (NATSISS) in previously published work (Biddle and Swee 2012; Biddle 2014; Biddle 2015). Rather, this discussion has attempted to highlight that there are Indigenous-specific notions of development that need to be taken into account when trying to understand the education decision, that the returns to education should be measured across both subjective and objective measures, and that there is likely to be variation across and within countries in terms of what is valued and prioritised when Indigenous peoples make development decisions for themselves.

Note

1 www.pmc.gov.au/indigenous-affairs/closing-gap.

References

Altman, J. C. (2009). *Beyond closing the gap: Valuing diversity in Indigenous Australia*, Citeseer.

Becker, G. S. (1964). *Human capital: A theoretical analysis with special reference to education*. New York: Columbia University Press.

Becker, G. S. (1994). Human capital revisited. *Human capital: A theoretical and empirical analysis with special reference to education* (3rd edition). Chicago: The University of Chicago Press: 15–28.

Biddle, N. (2014). "Measuring and analysing the wellbeing of Australia's Indigenous population." *Social Indicators Research* **116**(3).

Biddle, N. (2015). "Indigenous income, wellbeing and behaviour: Some policy complications." *Economic Papers: A Journal of Applied Economics and Policy* **34**(3): 139–149.

Biddle, N. and H. Swee (2012). "The relationship between wellbeing and indigenous land, language and culture in Australia." *Australian Geographer* **43**(3): 215–232.

Calma, T. (2010). "Chalmers oration: What's needed to close the gap." *Rural Remote Health* **10**(3): 1586.

Dodson, M. (1998). "Linking international standards with contemporary concerns of Aboriginal and Torres Strait Islander peoples." In S. Pritchard (ed.), *Indigenous peoples, the United Nations and human rights*. NSW, The Federation Press: 18–29.

Durie, M. (2006). "Measuring Māori wellbeing." *New Zealand Treasury Guest Lecture Series* **1**.

Guimond, E. (1999). "Ethnic mobility and the demographic growth of Canada's aboriginal populations from 1986 to 1996." *Current Demographic Trends*: 190–191.

Hall, G. H. and H. A. Patrinos (2012). *Indigenous peoples, poverty, and development*, Cambridge, UK: Cambridge University Press.

Haozous, E. A., C. J. Strickland, J. F. Palacios and T. G. A. Solomon (2014). "Blood politics, ethnic identity, and racial misclassification among American Indians and Alaska Natives." *Journal of Environmental and Public Health* 2014.

Keeley, B. (2007). *Human capital: How what you know shapes your life*. Paris: Organisation for Economic Co-operation and Development (OECD).

Kukutai, T. (2004). "The problem of defining an ethnic group for public policy: Who is Maori and why does it matter." *Social Policy Journal of New Zealand* **23**: 86–108.

Kukutai, T. and J. Taylor (2013). "Postcolonial profiling of indigenous populations. limitations and responses in Australia and New Zealand." *Espace populations sociétés. Space populations societies* (2012/1): 13–27.

Kukutai, T. and M. Walter (2015). "Recognition and indigenizing official statistics: Reflections from Aotearoa New Zealand and Australia." *Statistical Journal of the IAOS* **31**(2): 317–326.

Kukutai, T. and M. Webber (2017). "Ka Pū Te Ruha, Ka Hao Te Rangatahi: Maori identities in the twenty-first century." In A. Bell, V. Elizabeth, T. McIntosh, and M. Wynyard (Eds.), *A land of milk and honey? Making sense of Aotearoa New Zealand* (pp. 71–82). Auckland, New Zealand: Auckland University Press.

Kukutai, T. H. (2007). "White mothers, brown children: Ethnic identification of Maori-European children in New Zealand." *Journal of Marriage and Family* **69**(5): 1150–1161.

Liebler, C. A. (2018). "Counting America's First Peoples." *The ANNALS of the American Academy of Political and Social Science* **677**(1): 180–190.

Malenfant, E. C., S. Coulombe, E. Guimond and A. Lebel (2012). "Intragenerational ethnic mobility of aboriginal peoples in Canada: Results from the 2001 and 2006 censuses record linkage." San Francisco: Population Association of America.

Markham, F. and N. Biddle (2017). "Indigenous population change in the 2016 Census." 2016 CAEPR Census Paper Series 1.

Markham, F. and N. Biddle (2018). "Indigenous identification change between 2011 and 2016: evidence from the Australian Census Longitudinal Dataset." *CAEPR Topical Issue* **1**(2018).

Martinez Cobo, J. R. (1987). "Definition of indigenous populations." In Study of the problem of discrimination against indigenous populations, Chapter 5. New York: UN DESA.

McSweeney, K. and S. Arps (2005). "A 'demographic turnaround': the rapid growth of the indigenous populations in Lowland Latin America." *Latin American Research Review* **40**(1): 3–29.

Nussbaum, M. (2000). *Women and human development: a study in human capabilities*, Cambridge, UK: Cambridge University Press.

Pearson, N. (2005). "Freedom, capabilities and the Cape York reform agenda." *Viewpoint*, October.

Sen, A. (2001). *Development as freedom*, Oxford, UK: Oxford Paperbacks.

Sen, A. (2004). *Rationality and freedom*, Cambridge, MA: Harvard University Press.

Sirén, A. H. (2007). "Population growth and land use intensification in a subsistence-based indigenous community in the Amazon." *Human Ecology* **35**(6): 669–680.

Te Whāiti, P., M. B. McCarthy and A. Durie (1997). *Mai I Rangiâatea: Maori wellbeing and development*. Auckland, NZ: Auckland University Press.

Yap, M. and E. Yu (2016). "Operationalising the capability approach: developing culturally relevant indicators of indigenous wellbeing–an Australian example." *Oxford Development Studies* **44**(3): 315–331.

2 The Human Capital Model and its application to Indigenous peoples

Chapter 1 introduced the three main concepts for this book: who is Indigenous; what is the Human Capital Model; and what are our main measures of Indigenous development. Importantly, the chapter discussed the complexity around many of these concepts and the way in which the assumptions we make about them matter. In this chapter, I outline the Human Capital Model in more detail, focusing on its applicability for understanding Indigenous development and decision making.

Although the HCM has been quite influential in education research and policy making, it has also been recognised that, at least under the basic specification presented above, it has a number of limitations. The first of these is whether education enhances productivity directly (as assumed in the HCM), or instead acts as a signalling or screening device whereby already productive workers are identified (e.g. Arrow, 1973).

Under the alternative specification, employers assume that those with a higher innate ability find education easier (or less costly) and are therefore more likely to invest heavily in education than those who find education a struggle. An employer is therefore more likely to hire a person with relatively high levels of education, not because the education they have undergone has made them more productive, but because it has demonstrated that they were more productive in the first place.

Whether or not it is human capital or screening/signalling that is driving the differences in earnings has important implications for some aspects of policy development. If governments are trying to decide on the level of investment they make in education or the type of education to focus on, then under the HCM across-the-board increases in education lead to higher economy-wide productivity: therefore there is a much stronger argument for government provision of education. Under a signalling/screening model, however, education only affects relative earnings and therefore economy-wide increases in education have no or little effect on the overall size of the economy. The distinction is less important, however, when considering underinvestment in Indigenous education, where in most countries the Indigenous population is not large enough for improvements in Indigenous education to negatively impact on the outcomes of the non-Indigenous population.

There are, however, a number of more important limitations to the model that do need to be considered when applying the model to the decisions of Indigenous peoples. Specifically:

- Are there economic returns to education for Indigenous peoples?
- Are there social returns that are more relevant for the education decision?
- Are there costs that outweigh these benefits?
- What is the level of ability that Indigenous peoples bring to education? and
- Are there alternative forms of education (outside of the mainstream, Western system) that have competing or complementary returns?

The premise of this book, and the argument for using the HCM, is that the answers to the above questions will help explain the education decision of Indigenous peoples in different contexts. Importantly, the answers will also help demonstrate why Indigenous peoples are less likely to engage in formal education than their non-Indigenous counterparts in many (though importantly not all) circumstances. The remainder of this chapter will summarise some of the existing research on these questions, whereas the Chapter 3 will present new data on some of the specific aspects in detail.

The economic returns to education

A fundamental question for Indigenous policy developments is whether there are positive economic returns to education, and whether these economic returns vary relative to comparable non-Indigenous populations. One of the insights from the HCM is that for explaining the education decision, the differences in income, employment or other economic measures between Indigenous and non-Indigenous peoples with similar levels of education is not relevant. To be very clear, these differences matter greatly when trying to understand discrimination or other forms of inequity in labour markets. However, when understanding the education decision, what matters most are the differences in outcomes between an Indigenous person who has completed that particular form of education and an otherwise comparable Indigenous person who has not. It is the marginal difference that matters, or the comparison with the counterfactual, not the average outcomes.

While there are significant challenges in measuring causal impact (remember the signalling/productivity discussion earlier), almost exclusively the research shows that there are large differences in employment and income by education for Indigenous peoples. This has been shown in a developed country context (Biddle 2006; Stephens 2010; Pendakur and Pendakur 2011; Baum, Ma et al. 2013) as well as for Indigenous peoples in low and middle income countries, particularly in Latin America (Hall 2005; Hall and Patrinos 2012).

The relationship between employment and income for the Australian population is summarised in Figure 2.1 for Indigenous males and females and Figure 2.2 for their non-Indigenous counterparts. Focusing on the 15–64 year old population (including those who were studying at the time), results are given for five education groupings:

- Those who haven't completed Year 12 and do not have any post-school qualifications (No Year 12 – No quals).
- Those who haven't completed Year 12 but do have non-degree, post-school qualifications (No Year 12 – Other quals).
- Those who have completed Year 12 but do not have any post-school qualifications (Year 12 – No quals).
- Those who have completed Year 12 and have non-degree, post-school qualifications (Year 12 – Other quals).
- Those with a Bachelor degree or above, regardless of their Year 12 completion (Degree).

There are three stylised facts from these results. First, higher levels of education are associated with a higher probability of employment for both Indigenous males and females. Second, Indigenous males with lower levels of education have a greater employment probability than females with similar levels of education, but the gender gap is essentially zero at the upper end of the education distribution. The third stylised fact is that the (within-sex) employment disparities by Indigenous status are much greater at the lower end of the education distribution, with no real gap for males for those with a degree, and a higher employment probability for Indigenous females with a degree than non-Indigenous females.

Putting this (and the rest of the literature) another way, it would not appear that the employment and income benefits of education are any lower for Indigenous populations than they are for non-Indigenous

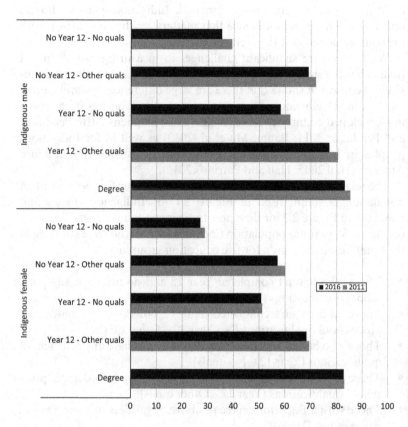

Figure 2.1 Percentage of working age population employed, by education –
Indigenous males and females, 2011 and 2016

populations. Indeed, in many cases they appear to be higher. This has
two implications. First, for those governments and communities that
are focused on improving the economic circumstances of Indigenous
peoples, investment in education is a key policy imperative. Second, other
explanations are required for explaining low education participation.

The social and other returns to education

The basic HCM assumes that a person's utility is determined mainly by
their income, and if discounted future additional income is higher than
the cost of education, then people will invest in education. There are
also a number of other outcomes that are likely to be associated with

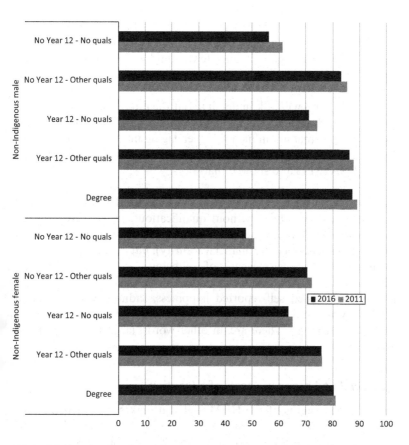

Figure 2.2 Percentage of working age population employed, by education –
non-Indigenous males and females, 2011 and 2016

higher education levels that people may take into account when deciding whether or not to invest in education. Although there are indirect effects that operate via income, education may also have direct effects on things like health, the schooling of one's children and the ability to plan fertility decisions (Wilson, Wolfe et al. 2005, Conti, Heckman et al. 2010).

There is very strong evidence for there being health benefits of education for Indigenous peoples, with those Indigenous Australians (for example) who have completed relatively high levels of education much less likely to report their health as being fair or poor, as well as being less likely to report a range of long-term health conditions (Biddle

2006). There are similar findings in other comparable countries (King, Smith et al. 2009). Similarly, those Indigenous females with relatively high levels of education have been shown to be better able to manage their own fertility decisions, have fewer children on average and have those children at a later age (Bremner, Bilsborrow et al. 2009; Biddle and Crawford 2015).

The Chapter 3 will talk in detail about the intergenerational aspects of education, but there are also likely to be a number of Indigenous-specific factors that are influenced by engaging in formal education. In 2012, I and a colleague (Biddle and Cameron 2012) analysed data from the 2008 NATSISS and showed that:

> Those with relatively high levels of education tend to have better outcomes than those without qualifications or who drop out of school. Differences tend to be greatest for the economic variables (employment, income, financial security), but are also present for a number of broader measures of wellbeing.

The latter included self-reported happiness, sadness, involvement in cultural events and feeling able to have a say within the community on important issues. There are, in other words, large social returns to education.

The social and economic costs of education

One of the strengths of the HCM is that it makes it explicit that not only are there likely to be benefits of education for the individual and their family, but there are also costs. What's more, these costs are often felt in the present, whereas the benefits are gained in the (distant) future. The standard HCM takes into account two main sets of costs – direct costs and opportunity costs.

The direct costs of education, as the name implies, are the fees paid to participate in a particular form of education. In some countries (particularly Australia, Canada and New Zealand), the fees for most forms of education are relatively low for Indigenous peoples or, in the case of university education, only need to be paid back through the tax system once a person's earnings are above a certain threshold (known as an income contingent loan; Chapman 2006). In the US, early childhood and school education tends to be freely provided in a local area, though the quality of public schools (real or perceived) varies quite considerably by geography and the cost of obtaining a good education is transferred to the housing market (Reeves 2018). Of course, the university system in the US is notoriously and increasingly expensive (McGettigan 2013), though there are a number of scholarships available for those from low income backgrounds. In low and middle income country contexts, direct costs of education vary quite substantially, although so too does the quality of education received (Levy and Schady 2013).

So, direct costs can be important. But for many potential students, the direct costs of education aren't the largest set of costs that are faced. Especially for adults considering late secondary or post-secondary education, the opportunity cost of studying can be many times higher. It takes time to engage in education. Lectures need to be attended, assignments need to be written, exams need to be prepared for. If a person is spending time engaging in those activities, then that leaves less time to engage in paid employment. The wages that a person would receive if they weren't studying is then the opportunity cost of that degree. For a full-time student with a Bachelor degree, this can be quite high.

The opportunity costs of education can often have very different patterns compared with the direct costs. While the direct costs of education relative to a person's financial circumstances go down the higher their socioeconomic position, the opposite occurs for the opportunity costs of education. It is those who are valued as being most productive in the labour market for whom the opportunity cost of education is highest. Furthermore, during times of economic uncertainty, a fixed direct cost of education can seem like more of a barrier. The opportunity costs of education tend to vary in the opposite direction, with boom times leading to the largest costs (and therefore lower rates of participation).

Given the large wage disparities between many Indigenous peoples and their non-Indigenous counterparts (as will be documented later in this book), it is likely that the opportunity costs of education for Indigenous peoples are relatively low. However, in certain circumstances there is very high demand for the labour of Indigenous peoples with specific sets of skills, for example for governments and resource extraction companies attempting to meet their social responsibilities (Langton 2013). This can mean that the opportunity costs of education in certain circumstances might be quite high.

By participating in education, students also forgo opportunities to supplement their family's income and resources through alternative livelihood-generating activities. For example, a large number of Indigenous peoples, particularly but not exclusively in remote areas, have been shown to continue to engage in hunting, fishing and gathering, with strong evidence for a positive association with subjective wellbeing and economic security (Biddle and Swee 2012). If these activities are not accommodated within the schooling system, then there is a trade-off that needs to be made in making the decision to attend school or post-school education.

Economic costs aren't the only costs experienced by Indigenous peoples (or others) when making the education decision. It is likely that a student's current social situation is also important in influencing their behaviour. Specifically, children who have positive attitudes to school are more likely to intend completing Year 12 and are also more likely to actually do so (Khoo and Ainley 2005).

Internationally, there are a number of papers that consider the different and generally higher costs of education for minority groups. Akerlof and Kranton (2002), as well as Austen-Smith and Fryer Jr (2005) consider situations where a minority subgroup faces a trade-off between higher wages and the social stigma an individual receives from their own subgroup. This stigma results from expending time in an activity associated with the majority group. These economic models follow a large body of sociological and ethnographic evidence that proposes that certain population subgroups view effort in education as a form of 'selling-out'.

There are likely to be specific aspects of these social costs for Indigenous peoples. According to a detailed ethnographic study of the Indigenous Australian population in an inner-city area, 'there appeared to be less shame in running the streets than fighting a losing classroom battle', and 'resisting school offered a sense of solidarity, another individual struggling against the wider oppression and rejecting success offered by the system under its own terms' (Munns and McFadden 2000).

When school is not enjoyable or is a place of conflict (with peers or with those in a position of authority), this can be conceptualised as a cost that individuals face to attend. While this is likely to be faced by the general population of students to some extent, students who experience bullying at school as a result of their ethnicity, gender, sexuality, disability or other characteristics are likely to face greater costs of attending school (Dupper 2013).

Ability and the education decision

Education is in many ways less costly for those with higher levels of ability (as valued in that type of education). In order to achieve a certain grade or result in a particular education setting, those with higher levels of academic ability require less of a time investment. This frees up time for work, leisure, or social interactions, all of which have large benefits to the individuals. Furthermore, undertaking a particular level of education has far lower benefits if that person doesn't receive a degree, diploma, or certificate for completion (known as the sheepskin effect – Jaeger and Page (1996)). Those with higher levels of academic ability have more certainty as to whether they will actually be able to complete that degree, meaning that the *ex ante* returns are higher.

I mentioned at the start of the book that there is no evidence or plausible theory to suggest that Indigenous peoples have lower aptitude than non-Indigenous peoples (Reich 2018). There is likely to be variation within Indigenous populations, just as there is variation in the non-Indigenous population. There are brilliant mathematicians,[1] artists, writers, social scientists, medical doctors, legal theorists, educators, etc. from all Indigenous peoples across the world. However, it should also be noted that the latent ability of many Indigenous peoples may not be perceived in the same way as their non-Indigenous counterparts, because most of the teachers and lecturers that make judgements about the ability of students don't come from an Indigenous background themselves, and are likely to suffer from what is known as the affinity bias (where we judge people more favourably if they are like us).

Equally important is the consistent experience of Indigenous peoples across the world in lacking access to high quality, early childhood education that would allow this ability to be developed and applied to formal education. In Australia, for example, the original Closing the Gap targets set in 2008 had full access to preschool for Indigenous Australians in remote areas as one of the six targets. This target was not met. Furthermore, according to the Australian Early Development Census (AEDC), Indigenous children are assessed as being developmentally vulnerable at more than twice the rate of non-Indigenous children in their first year of full-time schooling.[2] It is these two factors (lack of recognition of the ability of Indigenous peoples and lack of investment in early childhood education) that are likely to explain any differences in ability between Indigenous and non-Indigenous peoples in later childhood and adulthood.

Indigenous specific education

Although not explicitly so, much of the research and data that I have been discussing up until now has focused on the costs and benefits of formal, mainstream education. That is, early learning services, schools and tertiary education providers that have been set up by non-Indigenous peoples or non-Indigenous institutions, where the majority of those who attend are non-Indigenous, and the majority of instruction is not Indigenous specific. These forms of education cannot exclude Indigenous peoples either implicitly or explicitly, as they are pathways to economic success in the vast majority of societies that Indigenous peoples live in. However, there are other forms of education that many Indigenous people engage in, that may be seen as either a complement or supplement to mainstream education.

If the benefits of these alternative forms of education are higher or if the costs of participating are lower, then the HCM and common sense would suggest that Indigenous peoples would engage with these forms of education as opposed to more mainstream ones. I will return to this issue in more detail in Chapter 5.

Notes

1 See, for example, the work of Professor Robert Megginson of the University of Michigan, and his work not only in mathematics research, but also in publicising and developing the mathematical ability of other Native Americans; https://lsa.umich.edu/math/people/faculty/meggin.html.
2 www.aedc.gov.au/about-the-aedc/aedc-news/article/2016/03/08/progress-towards-narrowing-the-gap.

References

Akerlof, G. A. and R. E. Kranton (2002). "Identity and schooling: Some lessons for the economics of education." *Journal of Economic Literature*: 1167–1201.
Arrow, K. J. (1973). *Information and economic behavior*, Cambridge, MA: Harvard University Press.
Austen-Smith, D. and R. G. Fryer Jr (2005). "An economic analysis of 'acting white'". *The Quarterly Journal of Economics*: 551–583.
Baum, S., J. Ma and K. Payea (2013). *Education pays, 2013: The benefits of higher education for individuals and society*. Trends in Higher Education Series. College Board.
Biddle, N. (2006). "Health benefits of education in Australia: Indigenous/non-Indigenous comparisons." *The Economic and Labour Relations Review* **17**(1): 107–141.
Biddle, N. (2006). "Is it worth going to school? Variation in the predicted benefits of education for Indigenous Australians." *Australian Journal of Labour Economics* **9**(2): 172–200.
Biddle, N. and T. Cameron (2012). "The benefits of Indigenous education: Data findings and data gaps." In B. Hunter and N. Biddle (eds), *Survey analysis for indigenous policy in Australia*. Canberra: ANU ePress, 103–123.
Biddle, N. and H. Crawford (2015). "The changing Aboriginal and Torres Strait Islander population: Evidence from the 2006–11 Australian Census Longitudinal Dataset." CAEPR Indigenous Population Project 2011 Census Paper 18.

Biddle, N. and H. Swee (2012). "The relationship between wellbeing and indigenous land, language and culture in Australia." *Australian Geographer* **43**(3): 215–232.

Bremner, J., R. Bilsborrow, C. Feldacker and F. L. Holt (2009). "Fertility beyond the frontier: Indigenous women, fertility, and reproductive practices in the Ecuadorian Amazon." *Population and Environment* **30**(3): 93–113.

Chapman, B. (2006). "Income contingent loans for higher education: International reforms." *Handbook of the Economics of Education* **2**: 1435–1503.

Conti, G., J. Heckman and S. Urzua (2010). "The education-health gradient." *American Economic Review* **100**(2): 234–238.

Dupper, D. R. (2013). *School bullying: New perspectives on a growing problem*, New York: Oxford University Press.

Hall, G. (2005). *Indigenous peoples, poverty and human development in Latin America*, Springer.

Hall, G. H. and H. A. Patrinos (2012). *Indigenous peoples, poverty, and development*, Cambridge, MA: Cambridge University Press.

Jaeger, D. A. and M. E. Page (1996). "Degrees matter: New evidence on sheepskin effects in the returns to education." *The Review of Economics and Statistics*: 733–740.

Khoo, S. T. and J. Ainley (2005). "Attitudes, intentions and participation." *LSAY Research Reports*: 45.

King, M., A. Smith and M. Gracey (2009). "Indigenous health part 2: the underlying causes of the health gap." *The Lancet* **374**(9683): 76–85.

Langton, M. (2013). *Boyer lectures 2012: The quiet revolution: Indigenous people and the resources boom*, Sydney, AU: HarperCollins Australia.

Levy, S. and N. Schady (2013). "Latin America's social policy challenge: Education, social insurance, redistribution." *Journal of Economic Perspectives* **27**(2): 193–218.

McGettigan, A. (2013). *The great university gamble: Money, markets and the future of higher education*, London: Pluto Press.

Munns, G. and M. McFadden (2000). "First chance, second chance or last chance? Resistance and response to education." *British Journal of Sociology of Education* **21**(1): 59–75.

Pendakur, K. and R. Pendakur (2011). "Aboriginal income disparity in Canada." *Canadian Public Policy* **37**(1): 61–83.

Reeves, R. V. (2018). *Dream hoarders: How the American upper middle class is leaving everyone else in the dust, why that is a problem, and what to do about it.* Washington, DC: Brookings Institution Press.

Reich, D. (2018). *Who we are and how we got here: Ancient DNA and the new science of the human past.* Oxford, UK: Oxford University Press.

Stephens, B. J. (2010). "The determinants of labour force status among Indigenous Australians." *Australian Journal of Labour Economics* **13**(3): 287.

Wilson, K., B. Wolfe and R. Haveman (2005). "The role of expectations in adolescent schooling choices: Do youths respond to economic incentives?" *Economic Inquiry* **43**(3): 467–492.

3 The determinants of Indigenous human capital development and barriers to development

American Indian and Alaska Natives in the US labour market

In the Chapter 2, I presented a range of existing papers that showed that the differences in economic outcomes between individual Indigenous peoples by education are quite high. Much of this research, however, is a number of years old and may not hold in the current economic environment (or taking into account the growth and changing characteristics of the Indigenous populations mentioned even earlier). More specifically, as far as I am aware, there is no recent paper that looks at the relationship between education and economic outcomes for the American Indian and Alaskan Native (AIAN) population in the US, the largest Indigenous population in a developed country.

In this section, I present some new analysis of unit record data from Dataset A of the 2012–2016 American Community Surveys (ACSs). This pooled dataset has information on around 120,000 people who report their race as AIAN population either alone, or in combination with another race. As mentioned earlier, the concept of race is very problematic, especially when analysing the outcomes of Indigenous peoples (Sussman 2014). However, that is the way in which questions are framed and data is collected in the US Census and the ACS. Individuals from all 50 US States/Territories and Puerto Rico were interviewed in five waves of data collection – 2012, 2013, 2014, 2015 and 2016.

I look at two main outcomes of interest – the probability of being employed,[1] and personal income for those who are employed. I first look at the outcomes for these two variables for those who identify as AIAN (either alone or in combination with some other race) compared with those who report 'White' as their only race and who do not report a Hispanic ethnicity (henceforth referred to as non-Hispanic whites – NHW). In this analysis, I control for a person's age and whether or not they were born overseas. I then look at how these two outcomes vary for

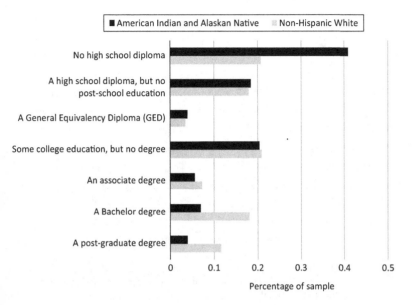

Figure 3.1 Education levels for American Indian and Alaskan Natives and non-Hispanic White population, 2012–2016, aged 15 plus

adults based on the person's highest level of education, collapsed into seven categories:

- no high school diploma;
- a high school diploma, but no post-school education;
- a General Equivalency Diploma (GED);
- some college education, but no degree;
- an Associate degree;
- a Bachelor degree; and
- a post-graduate degree.

The distribution of these education categories for our two populations of interest is given in Figure 3.1. As you can see, the AIAN population is much more likely to have not completed a high school diploma, but are substantially less likely to have an Associate degree or higher qualification.

Controlling for age only,[2] there are large differences in income and employment between AIAN and the NHW population. For males, the probability of a NHW aged 40 in 2016 being employed is 0.873. For an

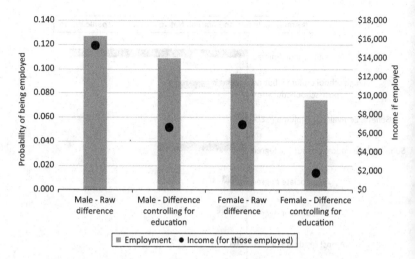

Figure 3.2 Differences in employment between American Indian and Alaskan Natives and non-Hispanic White population, with and without education controls

AIAN male (of the same age), the predicted probability is 0.746, or a difference of 0.127. This is large, statistically significant and likely to lead to very different labour market experiences across the lifecourse. For females, the difference in employment probabilities of 0.096 is smaller (0.789 and 0.693) but still large and statistically significant. There are similarly large differences in income for those who are employed.[3]

For males, predicted income for an employed NHW respondent in the sample is $63,343 compared with $48,077 for AIAN respondents. This difference of $15,265 is a little under a third of the size of the AIAN predicted income. For females, the differences are once again smaller but still statistically significant. At $6,891 (around one-fifth of the AIAN population, or $35,404 compared with $42,295).

These aren't causal estimates or direct evidence of labour market discrimination. There are many things that aren't controlled for in the model that are likely to impact on employment and income. Returning to the discussion in Chapter 1, this includes preferences for engagement in the labour market relative to other livelihood-generating activities. However, whatever the reasons, AIAN are less likely to be employed and have lower incomes if employed than the NHW population. To what extent do education differences explain these differences? This is summarised in Figure 3.2, which has the differences in employment and income for an AIAN and a NHW with the same level of education.[4]

For both males and females, and for income and employment, the difference between AIAN and NHW is much lower when education is controlled for than when it isn't. This is particularly the case for income for AIAN females, where the difference decreases from $6,891 without controlling for education to $1,722 when education is controlled for.

So, what does the data from the ACS show? Essentially education explains some, but not all of the economic differences between the AIAN and NHW populations. There are some differences by gender (and similar patterns have also been found in Australia) with gaps between AIAN males and females, but larger gaps with the NHW population for males that don't decline by as much once education is controlled for. However, based on the observational data investments in human capital will likely reduce differences in economic development between the Indigenous and non-Indigenous populations of the US, but differences will still remain.

The sources of this remaining variation are of course of key interest for policy makers. Some of the remaining difference is likely to be due to discrimination in the labour market. While I wasn't able to find direct evidence for the US, there is strong evidence from both self-reported (Biddle 2013; Biddle, Howlett et al. 2013) and experimental data (Booth, Leigh et al. 2012) in Australia that Indigenous Australians do experience labour market discrimination. There is also an enormous amount of research on other ethnic groups in the US (Altonji and Blank 1999; Bertrand and Mullainathan 2004; Neumark 2016).

In addition to the impact of labour market discrimination, location is likely to impact on the employment and income of the AIAN population. This is a complicated methodological question, because where someone lives is partly a choice (based on a range of economic, social and cultural characteristics), but also a choice that is made under significant constraints. However, from a purely observational perspective, when I run a similar analysis to the above holding constant the area in which a person lives (using what is known as a fixed effects model), the difference between the Indigenous population and the rest of the population declines, but is still present.

A final potential explanation for the remaining gap is that the education levels for the AIAN might be different in unobserved ways from the education levels for the NHW population. Looking at post-school education, for example, not all colleges are the same. There is some evidence that there are greater returns to highly selective colleges in the US (Dale and Krueger 2014), particularly for minority groups (though unfortunately there are no causal estimates for Indigenous peoples specifically). That is not to say that there aren't also additional benefits from some of the educational institutions that Indigenous peoples attend (a point that will be returned to in later chapters). However, in the labour market at least, it is likely that there are unobserved differences not picked up in the ACS.

The intergenerational effects and determinants of education

The previous set of data showed that there were large differences by education in the labour market outcomes of American Indian and Alaskan Natives in the ACS. To understand the education decision, however, we need to go back earlier in the lifecourse to when many long-term education decisions are being made. One set of data we can use for this is the Longitudinal Survey of Australian Youth, also known as the LSAY.

There were around 331 Indigenous children aged 15 in 2009 who took part in the LSAY, for whom we have information on whether they were either a Year 12 student in 2012 or whether they had already completed Year 12 by then. We also have information on 6,228 non-Indigenous students to make comparisons against. Of those Indigenous students in the sample 50.7 per cent had at least one parent who had completed Year 12, compared with 68.8 per cent of non-Indigenous students (after weighting for undercount).

Building on the success of a number of Indigenous role models, many Indigenous leaders have advocated for a greater policy focus and a more evidence-based policy on improving the education outcomes of Indigenous children and youth. Chris Sarra has advocated a 'strong and smart' approach to Indigenous education, with high expectations and recognising the strengths and 'positive sense of what it means to be Aboriginal in contemporary Australian society'.[5] Ken Wyatt, the first Indigenous person elected to the Australian House of Representatives, made the following point in his maiden speech to Parliament: 'I used education as the way to change my life to get to where I am now and I believe that a quality education is the key to success for any young Australian.'

Both leaders, and many others, make the point that there not only needs to be high expectations of Aboriginal and Torres Strait Islander youth, but that there are barriers to achieving their education potential that are beyond their control. Some of these barriers are societal and structural. But, Indigenous students grow up with fewer role models who have been successful in formal schooling. This is known from many other data sources with the Australian Government's own reporting framework highlighting past education disparities as a potential explanation for the current education distribution (SCRGSP 2014).

What we haven't had, however, is robust estimates of the extent to which this environment translates into poorer education outcomes for children and youth. Here, the LSAY gives us some further clues.

According to the data, 64.9 per cent of Indigenous students without a parent who had completed Year 12 had either completed Year 12 themselves or were still a high school student. Compared with this, 73.3 per cent of those with a parent who had completed Year 12 had completed themselves or were still studying. For non-Indigenous students, the comparable figures were 72.1 per cent and 82.6 per cent, respectively.

These descriptive statistics point to three main conclusions, all of which are replicated later in this section using more detailed econometric regressions. First, there is a large and statistically significant gap in Year 12 completion or retention between Indigenous students with and without a parent who had completed Year 12. Second, the gap by parental education appears to be lower for the Indigenous population than it is for the non-Indigenous population (8.4 percentage points compared with 10.5 percentage points). Third, even comparing those with and without a parent who had completed Year 12, there is still a large gap in Year 12 completion and retention between Indigenous and non-Indigenous students. A non-Indigenous student with a parent who has completed Year 12 is still much more likely to have completed or still be completing high school than an Indigenous student whose parents have the same level of education.

The relationship between parental/carer and child education – what one might call the 'intergenerational education transmission', following Black and Devereux (2011) – is an important aspect of the HCM with implications for our understanding of dynamics within a society. There have been a number of empirical studies that have looked at variation in intergenerational education transmission across countries. Hertz, Jayasundera et al. (2007) looked at education transmission across 42 countries (unfortunately, not including Australia) and found correlations between parent and child schooling ranging from 0.66 in Peru to 0.10 in Ethiopia.

There have been fewer studies that have looked at variation in education transmission within countries. This is partly because institutional and policy settings are less likely to vary, one of the motivations for analysing intergenerational transmission of earnings or education. However, variation within countries can still be quite informative for our understanding of Human Capital and Indigenous Development. A relatively low transmission (which appears to be the case for the Indigenous population) implies greater social mobility within that group. On the other hand, it also might imply a lower return to the educational investment of the parent, a possible explanation for the relative underinvestment of that group.

Exploring the variation in the intergenerational transmission of education also has policy implications. If the transmission or correlation is high, then that supports interventions targeted towards the education of parents within the population. Those interventions would need to be properly evaluated, but we would expect flow-on effects for the education outcomes of children in such a population with high intergenerational transmission. Furthermore, a population with high transmission would be better suited to childhood interventions that target those from low education backgrounds. On the other hand, a low transmission population would be one that is better suited towards interventions that target children directly and that are not focused on low education families.

In this section of the book, I explore the three initial conclusions from the descriptive data above in more detail. I discuss the potential sources of intergenerational education transmission, using primarily a HCM, but also building on insights from a range of disciplines. I then look at the data and methodology used for this particular aspect of the analysis. Results are then presented across three subsequent subsections – early childhood education, intermediate school outcomes and school completion. I return to the issue of intergenerational transfer in the final chapter of this book, with some concluding comments and discussion on the implications of the findings.

Sources of intergenerational education transmission

The relationship between parental and child education is an inherently complex question requiring a multi-disciplinary approach. This is made even more complex when cultural and historical differences between settler and colonised populations are taken into consideration. While I have been using the HCM to understand the Indigenous education decision, I have also stressed a number of times that young children (or even teenagers) are unlikely to make a conscious cost–benefit calculation. Rather, many of the costs and benefits, particularly the economic ones, are likely to be mediated through their parents or carers.

Social norms within the family and community in which the child lives are also likely to influence the attendance decision. There are a number of ways in which parental education might affect child outcomes and why the strength of this relationship might vary. A source that is likely to be consistent across societies and through time is what Blanden (2013) labels genetic transmission. Higher ability parents are more likely to have higher ability children (as valued in education) who in turn find education easier or less costly and therefore end up with higher grades and more years of education. This is in many ways the argument made by Herrnstein and Murray (2010) in their highly controversial book on *The Bell Curve*. The problem with that text though, is that it has been used to focus on variation between populations (where innate ability is unlikely to vary) as opposed to within populations (where ability does vary). In his more recent book, Marks (2013) argues that 'cognitive ability has a considerably stronger influence than socioeconomic background on educational outcomes' (p. 234).

Although Blanden (2013) argues that this form of transmission is of less concern for policy (or less amenable to it), Sandel (2010) in his discussion of John Rawls' Theory of Justice makes the case that there is still some justification for intervention by the State in such circumstances. Furthermore, Blanden (2013) argues that given the cross-country variation in education transmission in his data, genetics cannot be the only explanation, or probably even the major one. Institutional factors must also matter.

Black and Devereux (2011) begin by noting that the presence of credit constraints makes such transmission much more likely. They state that 'if there are no credit constraints, and thus parents can borrow from their children's future earnings, each family will optimally invest in the human capital of their children' (p. 1502). Any elasticity between parent and child earnings in this situation is likely to be driven by heritability of ability. Credit constraints make such borrowing against future income much harder, creating a direct link between parental income, child education and (later) child income. The authors also discuss possible direct links between the education of parents and the education of children (above and beyond the relationship between parental income, credit constraints and child education). Specifically, they state that 'parental education may affect parental time allocation and the productivity of the parent in child-enhancing activities' and that 'education may change bargaining power in the household'.

The political economy of countries is also important. Piketty (2014), in his highly influential book *Capital in the Twenty-first Century*, discusses in detail the way in which those at the very top of the income distribution are much more likely to have children who themselves end up at the top of the distribution. His focus is in part on the effect of physical and financial capital as the driver for positive intergenerational income/wealth elasticity. However, he also notes that the relatively well off (and the relatively well educated) in many countries have used their position to enhance the probability of educational success for their children and later privileged position in the income/wealth hierarchy. In other words, intergenerational education transmission relates to the political economy and the ability of the well-educated to shape institutions to suit their offspring. Blanden (2013) also makes this point, stating that the 'extent and progressivity of educational investments are also likely to be influenced by the degree of inequality with society' and that if 'power resides with the median voter then greater inequality may lead to more redistributive spending ... but if it resides with the economic elite then the reverse might be the case' (p. 56).

Beyond economics, other disciplines have considered the causal mechanism for intergenerational education transmission. Perhaps the most fruitful line of enquiry (in contrast to economics) within sociology and education is the concept of cultural capital. According to Lareau (1987), this is the social and cultural elements of family life that help students successfully negotiate the school and university systems, particularly via parental involvement in the education production. Parents with higher levels of education face fewer social or psychic costs of doing so and hence the social costs of education for these students are lower.

There is also Indigenous-specific scholarship that tries to explain the education decision. Some of this work relates to the demand for education and resistance to the dominant culture as expressed through the school system and the workplace (Morgan 2012), whereas other research focuses on the supply-side and the inadequacy of school systems to adjust to Indigenous-specific needs and aspirations (Martin 2012). This supply- and demand-side is likely to influence the intergenerational transmission of education, through the different ways in which Indigenous parents engage with education depending on their own experiences (both positive and negative).

Results: Parental education and early childhood outcomes

In this sub-section, I explore the role of parental education in explaining early childhood outcomes among Indigenous children. Children who attend early childhood education have been found to be better off in terms of self-esteem and later social and emotional maturity, as well as being less likely to engage in criminal and antisocial behaviour, teen pregnancy or drug abuse (Hull and Edsall 2001). This can be partly ascribed to the effect of this education on later academic achievement, but also because of direct effects on social skills, maturity and self-confidence (Kronemann 1998).

The potential positive effects that early childhood education might have on future academic achievement and broader cognitive development are also important. Early childhood education can improve a child's school readiness and close some of the gap between 'at-risk' and other students in terms of cognitive development and school achievement. Most studies find that, in the short term, there are large effects on both achievement and IQ scores (Barnett 1998). Heckman, Stixrud et al. (2006) identify early childhood education as having its greatest effect on non-cognitive ability (motivation, persistence and self-esteem) as opposed to cognitive ability. Furthermore, Heckman, Stixrud et al. (2006) identify non-cognitive ability as being as important, if not more important than cognitive ability in explaining future outcomes like school completion and wage levels.

The outcome used in this part of the paper is the probability of a child aged 4 or 5 years old (as of August 2011) attending preschool. Excluded from the analysis are those that have already started full-time schooling, leaving 16,867 children in the 2011 Census Sample File upon which analysis is undertaken. Results are estimated across six models with the explanatory variables from each of the models outlined below:

- Model 1 – Indigenous status of the child is the only explanatory variable.
- Model 2 – Indigenous status, as well as sex, State/Territory of usual residence, child speaks a language other than English at home; changed usual residence in the previous year; number of children aged 0 to 3 in the household; number of other children aged 4 to 5 in the household; number of children aged 6 to 14 in the household; number of adults in the household; and whether there is more than one person per bedroom in the house.
- Model 3 – All variables from Model 2, as well as whether there is no one in the household who has completed Year 12 (low education household); and whether there is someone in the household who has completed a degree (high education household).
- Model 4 – All variables from Model 3, as well as whether the equivalised income of the household is zero or negative; income is low (between $1 and $399 per week); income is high ($1,000 or more per week); lives in a dwelling that is rented privately; lives in a household that is rented from the government or from a community organisation; and whether the household does not have anyone who is employed.
- Model 5 – All the variables from Model 4, estimated for Indigenous children only.
- Model 6 – All the variables from Model 4, estimated for non-Indigenous children only.

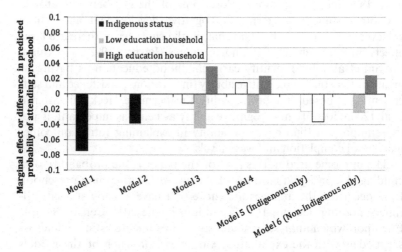

Figure 3.3 Relationship between preschool participation and household
          education/Indigenous status

Source: Customised calculation using the 2011 Census Sample File.

Results are summarised in Figure 3.3 through two sets of marginal
effects – or differences in the probability of attending preschool while
holding all else constant. The first set of marginal effects (for models
1 through to 4) is the difference in probability between an Indigenous
and non-Indigenous child. The second set of marginal effects (for
models 3 to 6) is the estimated association with household education,
as represented by whether the child lives in a low education household
(no one in the household has completed Year 12) or a high education
household (at least one person in the household has a degree). The base
case household for this second set of marginal effects is one in which
at least one person has completed Year 12, but no one has completed
a degree.

Figure 3.3 shows that there is a very large difference between
Indigenous and non-Indigenous children in preschool participation
(Model 1) that reduces, but is not eliminated when demography, geography and household context is controlled for (Model 2). However,
when household education is controlled for, the difference between
Indigenous and non-Indigenous children is no longer statistically significant. The association with household education may or may not be
causal – there are a number of other things correlated with education
that may affect preschool participation – but the result does show that

variation in education across the total population is likely to explain a large part of the difference between Indigenous and non-Indigenous children in preschool participation.

Household education is clearly important for the total population, and the non-Indigenous population as shown in Model 6. Compared with the base case child, non-Indigenous children in low education households have a lower probability of attending and those in high education households have a higher probability. The relationship for Indigenous children is, however, a little more complicated. While the coefficient for low education households is not statistically significant (with a sample size of 651 children this is perhaps not surprising), the size of the estimated marginal effect is comparable with non-Indigenous children.

The bigger difference between the two populations though is for the high education variable. Whereas those non-Indigenous children who live in a household where at least one person has a degree are significantly more likely to be attending preschool, there is no significant difference for Indigenous children. Leaving aside statistical significance, the coefficient is negative and the marginal effect large, showing that if anything those Indigenous children in high education households are slightly less likely to attend.

This finding may be a small sample issue – only 7.2 per cent of Indigenous children in the sample lived in a high education household. However, a similar result was found when analysing the 2006 CSF either separately or as part of a pooled sample. The result does, therefore, give *prima facie* evidence that the relationship between parental or carer education and preschool participation is not necessarily the same for Indigenous and non-Indigenous children.

Results: Parental education and intermediate school outcomes

Household education was only weakly associated with preschool participation among Indigenous Australian children in 2011. This is a potential explanation for the lower education transmission for this population documented in the introduction to this chapter. However, there are a number of other ways in which parental education might interact with child school completion. In this sub-section I use data from the 2012 Programme of International Student Assessments (PISA) to explore the relationship between Indigenous status, parental education and a set of intermediate school outcomes. These intermediate outcomes can be grouped into five types – cognitive ability (literacy and numeracy); socialisation; non-cognitive ability or executive control; social norms;

and expectations – with variables for each outlined below (standardised to have a mean of zero and standard deviation of one):

- Cognitive ability is measured using average values for the individual across three sets of test scores: reading, mathematics and science.
- Socialisation is measured using an index of a person's sense of belonging, which is calculated using a principal components analysis of student's response to nine questions about their school based on the extent to which they: feel like an outsider; make friends easily; belong at school; feel awkward at school; are liked by other students; feel lonely at school; feel happy at school; feel things are ideal at school; and are satisfied at school.
- Non-cognitive ability is measured by two variables, one on self-perceived control and the other on perseverance. Self-perceived control is measured by a principal components analysis of a student's response to six questions on whether: the child can succeed with enough effort; it is their choice whether they'll be good; problems prevent the child from putting effort into school; different teachers would make the student try harder; the student could perform well if they wanted; or they would perform poorly regardless. Perseverance is measured by a principal components analysis of five questions related to whether the student feels they: give up easily; remain interested; continue to perfection; and exceed expectations.
- Social norms are measured by an index of student attendance based on the frequency with which the student reports that they: are late for school; skip a whole school day; or skip classes within a school day.
- Expectations are measured by the highest level of education that the child expects to complete. They are measured in terms of years of education.

I begin the analysis by considering the relationship between Indigenous status and the intermediate outcomes outlined above. To do so, I construct four empirical models, each with Indigenous status as the main explanatory variable. These models are constructed in a similar way to those in the previous section, with an increasing number of explanatory variables as outlined below:

- Model 1 – Indigenous status of the student is the only explanatory variable.
- Model 2 – Indigenous status, as well as sex; school sector (Catholic, or Independent as opposed to government school); school location

(provincial or remote as opposed to major city); current school grade; whether or not the student attended preschool; the age at which they commenced school; whether or not they speak a language other than English at home; and whether or not they missed at least two months of school in a previous year.

- Model 3 – All variables from Model 2, as well as two sets of variables for the education characteristics of the student's mother and father that interact Year 12 completion with post-school qualifications (parent not at home, parent has not completed Year 12 or a qualification, parent has completed a non-degree qualification but not Year 12, parent has completed Year 12 and a non-degree qualification, and parent has a degree).

- Model 4 – All variables from Model 3, as well as an index of the wealth level of the family and two sets of variables for the employment characteristics of the student's mother and father (not employed, or employed part-time).

Results presented in Figure 3.4 give the Indigenous coefficient from each of the four models for the six dependent variables introduced earlier. That is, the estimated difference in the outcomes between an Indigenous youth and an otherwise identical non-Indigenous youth (while holding other characteristics constant). It should be kept in mind that the variables are calculated such that higher values represent more positive outcomes for the individual, with the first five scaled to have a mean of zero and a standard deviation of one. The last of the variables, the number of years of education that the individual expects to complete, ranges from 10 (leaving school before completing Year 10) to 15 (completing a degree). Across the sample, it has a mean value of 13.6 years and a standard deviation of 1.8.

While a standard cut-off for rejecting the null hypothesis that a coefficient is zero (or there is no relationship) is the 5 per cent level of significance, we can make an even stronger case in Figure 3.4 as all coefficients summarised are statistically significant at the 1 per cent level of significance. The size of the coefficients does decline when a wider range of variables are controlled for (moving from Model 1 through to Model 4) showing that some of the raw gap between Indigenous and non-Indigenous students is explained by observable characteristics. Nonetheless, even after controlling for parental education, wealth and employment (in Model 4), Indigenous students are still predicted to have lower cognitive ability, socialisation at school, non-cognitive ability, attendance and expectations for the future than non-Indigenous students.

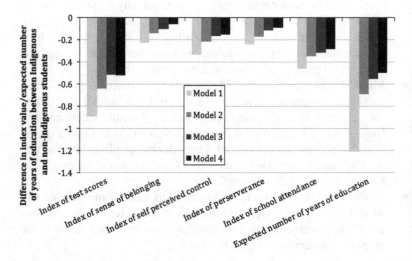

Figure 3.4 Relationship between intermediate school outcomes and
          Indigenous status
Source: Customised calculation using the Australian component of the 2012
PISA survey.

Looking across the figure, it is clear that Indigenous status is more
important for explaining variation in some outcome variables than
others. Focusing on the results for Model 4, Indigenous status has a
relatively large association for literacy/numeracy, expected years of education and, to a lesser extent, school attendance. However, it has a relatively small association with sense of belonging, perceived control and
perseverance.

More importantly from the perspective of this section, results
presented in Figure 3.4 show that parental education explains some, but
not all of the difference in intermediate outcomes between Indigenous
and non-Indigenous students. The main question for this chapter
though is whether the association with parental education and these
outcomes is as strong for the Indigenous population as it is for the non-
Indigenous population. I explore this in Figure 3.5 by presenting the
coefficient estimates for the parental education variables from Model 4,
estimated separately for Indigenous and non-Indigenous students. This
is analogous to Models 5 and 6 from the previous section, with a much
more detailed parental education specification.

Figure 3.5 summarises the results for the index of test scores. I focus
on this variable for two reasons. First, because of the potential effect

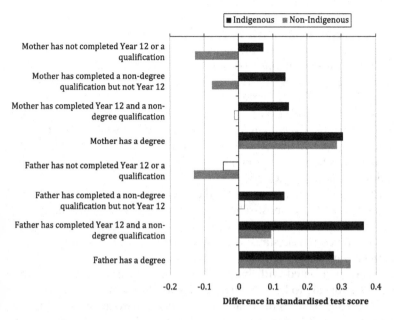

Figure 3.5 Relationship between test scores and detailed parental education, by Indigenous status

Source: Customised calculation using the Australian component of the 2012 PISA survey.

of literacy/numeracy on a range of other outcomes (Reeves, Venator et al. 2014). More importantly though, I focus on the relationship between literacy/numeracy and parental education because this was the variable that had the greatest gap between Indigenous and non-Indigenous students relative to its standard deviation and once observable characteristics were controlled. Results are presented as differences in predicted test scores relative to the omitted category (i.e. those who have completed Year 12 but do not have a post-school qualification), with those coefficients that are not statistically significant represented by the hollow bars.

Looking at the results for the non-Indigenous population to start with, there is a reasonably consistent relationship between parental education and student test scores. Keeping in mind that the omitted category is those who have completed Year 12 but do not have a post-school qualification, parents who have no qualification and who have not completed Year 12 are associated with the lowest test scores whereas parents with a degree (or higher) are associated with the highest test scores. In between, there is some variation by the gender of the parent, but in general higher levels of education of the parent are associated with higher test scores for the child.

This consistent finding was not the case for the Indigenous sample. There were 1,332 observations in this analysis, so sample size was not the main issue. Furthermore, at the upper end of the distribution, the association is as we'd expect. Children whose parents who have a degree tend to have relatively high test scores, as do those whose parents have completed Year 12 and who have a non-degree qualification. However, comparisons between the lower and middle part of the education distribution are more problematic.

Indigenous students whose mother has not completed Year 12 and who does not have a post-school qualification have a higher predicted test score than those whose mother has completed Year 12. For fathers, the difference is not statistically significant. Looking at this finding another way, among parents of Indigenous students, completing Year 12 is not associated with improved test scores for students and, for mothers, appears to be associated with worse test scores.

Figure 3.6 explores the relationship between parental education and a wider range of intermediate school outcomes. In order to simplify the analysis and to allow for tests of statistical significance, a more parsimonious specification is used. The four variables for the education levels of the student's mother and the four variables for the education levels of the student's father are collapsed into a single variable representing the highest level of education among both of the child's parents, expressed in terms of number of years. This variable is then interacted with the Indigenous status in order to allow for a formal statistical test of whether there are any differences in the (linear) relationship between parental education and intermediate school outcomes.

Results presented in Figure 3.6 for the non-Indigenous population are of the coefficient estimate for the parental education variable. Results for the Indigenous population are this coefficient plus the coefficient for the interaction term. The number of stars next to the variable name signifies the level of statistical significance for the interaction term. That is, whether or not the association between parental education and student education outcomes is different for Indigenous students compared with non-Indigenous students. Specifically, *** is for when the interaction term is statistically significant at the 1 per cent level of significance, ** is significant at the 5 per cent level of significance and * is significant at the 10 per cent level of significance. Those variables without any stars are for when the interaction term is not statistically significant even at the 10 per cent level of significance.

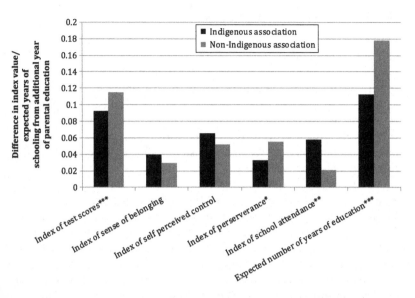

Figure 3.6 Relationship between intermediate school outcomes and parental education, by Indigenous status

Source: Customised calculation using the Australian component of the 2012 PISA survey.

The first set of results in Figure 3.6 confirms those from Figure 3.5. Yes, there is an association between test scores of Indigenous students and the education level of their parents. However, the size of the association is lower than it is for non-Indigenous students. This pattern was also found for one of the measures of non-cognitive ability (the index of perseverance) and for the expected number of years of education. In general, where there is a statistically significant difference, parental education has less of an association with Indigenous intermediate education outcomes than it does for non-Indigenous education outcomes.

The major exception to the above finding was for the index of school attendance. For this variable, an additional year of parental education was associated with a higher level of school attendance (that is, being less likely to be late for school, skip a whole school day or skip classes within a day). However, the magnitude of this association is reasonably small and is the lowest among all the outcome variables. The association for the Indigenous population was, however, much larger with an additional year of parental education associated with an increase in the index of 0.057 standard deviations.

Results: Parental education and school completion

In this sub-section, I explore the relationship between parental education and what I label Year 12 persistence (as outlined below). In particular, I consider three empirical questions: Are Indigenous students less likely to persist with Year 12 than non-Indigenous students once parental education is controlled for? Is the observed relationship between parental education and Year 12 persistence different for Indigenous and non-Indigenous students? And, how is the observed relationship between parental education and Year 12 persistence affected by controlling for intermediate school variables?

To answer these questions, I use data from Wave 4 of the 2009 cohort of the LSAY, collected in 2012. By this time, most students in the sample are aged 18 years. Of the 6,541 students still in the sample, 5,977 or 91.4 per cent were no longer at school. Of these, 5,321 or 89.0 per cent had completed Year 12, with the remaining 11.0 per cent having left school before completing Year 12. The outcome variable used in this part of the analysis combines current attendance and past completion into a measure of Year 12 persistence. It is calculated as the probability of not dropping out of school before completion with a value of 1 for those who were either still at school or have already completed Year 12 and a value of 0 for those who had dropped out before completing Year 12.

An important cautionary note is that the 6,541 students for whom we have information on Year 12 drop-out by Wave 4, represent only 45.9 per cent of the original 2009 cohort. Furthermore, this sample attrition is not random with Indigenous students in particular much more likely to drop out of LSAYs (Rothman 2009). In order to control for this (to the extent we can using observable information), I weight the data such that those observations still in the data in 2012 who would be more likely to have dropped out of the survey contribute more to the analysis. It should be noted though, that attrition due to unobservable characteristics is not possible to control for.

The relationship between parental education and Year 12 persistence is estimated across four models. All of these use Year 12 persistence as the dependent variable (estimated via maximum likelihood estimation of the probit model), with the following explanatory variables:

- Model 1 – Indigenous status as the only explanatory variable.
- Model 2 – Indigenous status and the highest level of education among both of the child's parents are the only explanatory variables.

- Model 3 – The two main explanatory variables are the highest level of education among both of the child's parents for the total population and the highest level of education among both of the child's parents separately for the Indigenous population. Additional explanatory variables are the child's demographic and family background (sex; whether or not they speak a language other than English at home); school sector at the age of 15 (Catholic, or Independent as opposed to government school); school location at the age of 15 (provincial or remote as opposed to major city); school grade at the age of 15; early school experience (whether or not the student attended pre-school; the age at which they commenced school; whether or not they missed at least two months of school before the age of 15); and standardised wealth at the age of 15.
- Model 4 – The variables from Model 3, as well as standardised test scores at the age of 15.

The results from Model 1 and 2 confirm that, while parental education is strongly and positively associated with Year 12 persistence, this does not explain all of the gap in Year 12 persistence between Indigenous and non-Indigenous students. Specifically, without controlling for parental education, the predicted probability of persistence for the Indigenous population is 0.692 compared with 0.793 for non-Indigenous students, a difference of 0.101. Estimated at the median value for parental education and holding parental education constant, the estimated difference in parental persistence between Indigenous and non-Indigenous students is still -0.098, virtually the same marginal affect as when parental education is not controlled for.

Figure 3.7 shows that one potential explanation for the size (if not the existence) of the gap between Indigenous and non-Indigenous Year 12 persistence is the smaller observed relationship with parental education for the former. As the dependent variable for this analysis is a probability as opposed to a continuous variable, results are presented as marginal effects. Specifically they are presented as the difference in the predicted probability of having a positive value for Year 12 persistence from an increase in parental education from 12 years (the second most common value in the sample) to 15 years (the most common value), while holding all other variables constant. Results are presented across models 3 and 4 (as outlined above) with the three stars for each indicating that the differences in the marginal effects for Indigenous and non-Indigenous students are statistically significant at the 1 per cent level of significance.

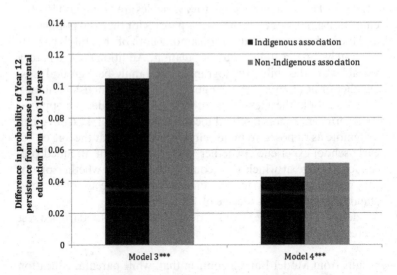

Figure 3.7 Relationship between Year 12 persistence and parental education, by Indigenous status

Source: Customised calculation using Wave 1 and 4 of the 2009 LSAY.

There are three main findings from the results presented in Figure 3.7. First, regardless of what is controlled for, there is a statistically significant difference for Indigenous students in Year 12 persistence between those with moderately educated parents and those with relatively high levels of education. Once again, this is not experimental data and does not prove causality. There may be other unobserved variables that are correlated with both parental education and Year 12 persistence. However, given the extensive range of controls included in the analysis, which includes well-validated measures of literacy and numeracy, this is strong *prima facie* evidence that the education of Indigenous parents has a strong effect on the education outcomes of their children.

The second thing to note from the results presented in Figure 3.7 though is that the size of the marginal effect is much smaller in Model 4 (when Maths, English and Science test scores are controlled for) compared with Model 3 (when they are not controlled for). For Indigenous students, the marginal effect is about 0.41 times as large in Model 4 compared with Model 3 and for non-Indigenous students it is about 0.45 times as large. This strongly implies that the association with the intermediate school variables documented in the previous sub-section is one way in which parental education impacts on eventual school outcomes. It is not the only explanation, as the size of the marginal effect is comparable to the student missing two or more months of school before the age of 15 or living in a provincial area as opposed to a major city. But, it is a part of the explanation for the observed bivariate relationship given in the introduction to this chapter.

The final point to note from Figure 3.7, and the one that is perhaps most relevant for this section, is that the estimated marginal effect of parental education is significantly and substantially smaller for Indigenous compared with non-Indigenous students. When test scores are not controlled for (in Model 3), the marginal effect for Indigenous students is about 0.91 times as large as it is for non-Indigenous students. When test scores are controlled for (in Model 4), it is about 0.83 times as large. Once again, while still important and relevant for policy formulation, intergenerational education transmission is smaller for Indigenous compared with non-Indigenous students.

Reflecting on the intergenerational effect of education

Schooling as experienced by many Indigenous peoples across the world is in most ways a Western or European institution. It is not surprising, therefore, that many Indigenous children and parents find it a negative experience and resist or withdraw (Martin 2012). Despite this, almost all Indigenous leaders, regardless of political perspective have argued for an urgent need to increase the number of Indigenous children and youth who are successfully engaged in early childhood, school and post-school education (Langton and Ma Rhea 2009; Behrendt, Larkin et al. 2012). This will only occur, however, if there is a breadth of evidence that identifies the enablers and barriers to education, rather than assuming that the fault or onus lies with Aboriginal and Torres Strait Islander children and families only.

Analysis presented in this section has focused on three main questions. First, are there differences between Indigenous and non-Indigenous students in education outcomes once parental education and other observable characteristics are controlled for? In general, the answer to this question is yes, though there are some exceptions. Most importantly, in the year before full-time schooling has commenced, an Indigenous child in the census is no less likely to be attending preschool than a non-Indigenous child with the same observable characteristics. Without controlling for these characteristics, there is still a large difference. But in terms of targeting policy, Indigenous status is less relevant, at least with regards to preschool participation.

Despite this exception related to preschool, the general finding from the analysis was that, by the age of 15, there was a large and statistically significant difference between Indigenous and non-Indigenous students in cognitive ability (literacy and numeracy); socialisation; non-cognitive ability or executive control; social norms; and expectations. Beyond the age of 15, despite the relatively small sample, there was still a statistically significant difference in Year 12 persistence. It is hard to think of any other characteristics that could be included in the model that: (a) are likely to affect these outcomes; (b) vary between Indigenous and non-Indigenous students; and (c) are amenable to targeting of government policy. This gives strong support for policies specifically focused on Indigenous students in supporting Indigenous education, ideally before the age of 15.

The second question guiding the analysis was whether there was an association between parental education and child education. In general, the evidence did support such intergenerational education transmission with one notable exception – relevant Indigenous children who lived in high-education households were no more likely to be attending preschool than those without a person in the household who had completed a degree. This may be because these households have the resources and need to access other forms of early childhood care with longer and more flexible hours. However, the fact that there was still a positive association for non-Indigenous children highlights the need for Indigenous early childhood education policy to be inclusive of households across the education distribution.

In general though, there was a positive association between parental education and child education outcomes for Indigenous students. This highlights the ongoing effect of past policy failures with regards to Indigenous education (failing to invest properly in the education of the parents of the current generation of Indigenous children is having an ongoing effect on that generation). However, it also gives a prediction for the difficulties likely to occur into the future as the current cohort of children and youth have children of their own. Ultimately though, it highlights a potential avenue for future policy trials. As has long been advocated (including by Schwab and Sutherland, 2001), investing in the education of Indigenous adults has the potential to improve not only their outcomes, but also the outcomes of their children. The current education policy focus in many countries is to tie Indigenous education to employment outcomes (this is enunciated in Australia, for example, by the review team headed by Twiggy Forrest, 2014). This has some merit, as achieving employment parity is also likely to have long-term benefits for Indigenous peoples and the taxpayer (Gray, Hunter et al. 2014). However, a focus on employment outcomes alone is too narrow and should not obscure the potential intergenerational effect of education.

This raises the final question in the analysis – whether the relationship between parental education and child education is as strong for the Indigenous population as it is for the non-Indigenous population. The answer to this question appears to be, no, it is not. This was hinted at with the preschool analysis discussed already. However, even when there was a significant association with parental education, the size of the predicted association tended to be lower for Indigenous children. This was true for three of the intermediate outcomes – cognitive ability, one measure of non-cognitive ability (perseverance) and education expectations. Most importantly, it was also true for Year 12 persistence.

There are a number of potential reasons why there might be a smaller level of intergenerational education transmission for Indigenous students. Unfortunately, none of these is testable using current data. First, it may be that the quality of education that Indigenous adults have received is lower than the quality for non-Indigenous adults. Second, it may be driven by the fact that Indigenous adults receive their education later in life than non-Indigenous adults (Biddle 2006) and therefore are less likely to be able to make use of that education when their child is young and at crucial developmental stages.

A final potential explanation, and one that builds on the strengths within the Indigenous community, is the general finding that Indigenous children receive care and support from a much greater network of family and community members (Morphy 2007). The implication of this is that relative to non-Indigenous children, the education of the community may matter more than the education of the child's family, and that many of the positive, Indigenous-led initiatives that are occurring (Perso and Hayward 2015) may be counterbalancing the relatively low levels of formal education discussed earlier.

New data and new evaluations are required to test the above explanations for a relatively low rate of intergenerational education transmission. Whatever the reason, however, the implication for policy is that education interventions for Indigenous students need to be spread across a much broader range of the education distribution than they would be for non-Indigenous students. There was, however, one exception to this finding. The relationship between parental education and student attendance was much stronger for Indigenous children than for non-Indigenous children. Here, the policy implications are reversed –Indigenous school attendance needs to have a particular focus on Indigenous children growing up in relatively low education households, as the difference between their attendance and that of children in high education households seems particularly large.

The quality and experience of schooling

The previous section highlighted the contribution of family-level factors to school attendance and completion for one particular Indigenous population. However, what happens in schools matters as well. In the HCM, individuals and their families make a decision to invest in schooling if the benefits of doing so outweigh the costs. The benefits (or returns) of attending school for a school period, or a day, week, month or year is likely to be much higher if the quality of that school is greater. In one of the seminal papers on this topic, Card and Krueger (1992) find that in the US 'men who were educated in states with higher-quality schools have a higher return to additional years of schooling. Rates of return are also higher for individuals from states with better-educated teachers and with a higher fraction of female teachers.'

While these authors were only able to use data on men (given the labour market conditions during the time), more recent estimates using richer data sources and therefore more robust estimation techniques confirm these findings. Specifically, Jackson, Johnson et al. (2015) show that:

> A 10% increase in per pupil spending each year for all 12 years of public school leads to 0.31 more completed years of education, about 7% higher wages, and a 3.2 percentage point reduction in the annual incidence of adult poverty; effects are much more pronounced for children from low-income families. Exogenous spending increases were associated with notable improvements in measured school inputs, including reductions in student-to-teacher ratios, increases in teacher salaries, and longer school years.

As far as I am aware, there is no study that specifically looks at the returns to school quality for any Indigenous peoples. This may have something to do with the lack of available longitudinal data, though this is changing as more and better linked datasets become available. However, given Jackson, Johnson et al. (2015) find that the returns are highest for those from low income families and we know that in all countries for which we have good data Indigenous peoples are concentrated in low income families, I would be surprised if the returns weren't as high as for the total population, or even higher.

We do, however, have reasonable data in Australia on a number of measures of school quality separately for the schools that a large sample of Indigenous children are attending. Specifically, a relevant aspect of PISA for the purposes of this discussion is that it systematically collects objective and subjective information from a representative sample of 15 year-old students, as well as principals across a wide (but random) selection of schools.

Several pieces of information can be obtained from PISA which can assist with the discussion in this section. Data relating to the Indigenous status of students and their socioeconomic background is available. As is school-level information on student/teacher ratios, capacity constraints, learning restrictions and parental expectations. Importantly this student- and school-level information can be linked. Specifically, we have data on 14,530 Australian students aged 15 years at the time of test. Of these, there were 2,807 Indigenous students (1,534 living in urban areas, 1,085 regional and 188 remote). This individual level data was merged with the School Principal question-naire, with students coming from 758 schools, with 3.7 Indigenous students on average. I calculated the weighted average of school or individual level characteristics separately for Indigenous and non-Indigenous students, taking into account the sample weights from the analysis.

So, what can we say about the schools of 15-year-old Indigenous students and those from low socioeconomic backgrounds based on the most recently available PISA, enumerated in 2015?

Student to teacher ratios

Firstly, I calculated student/teacher ratios by dividing the total number of students enrolled at a particular school by teachers reported to be currently on the staff of the school. While there is mixed evidence on the cost-effectiveness of reducing student/teacher ratios relative to other investments (Fryer 2017), there is reasonably strong evidence that some students do better with smaller class sizes.

In my calculations, teachers that were employed less than 90 per cent of the time for the full school year were considered part-time and given a value of 0.5. I then divide the total number of students by the total number of teachers in the school, keeping in mind that not all teachers will be teaching at a given point in time, so the actual class size that students experience are going to be quite different.

Looking at the schools which Indigenous students attend, there was an average of 13.5 students for every teacher. While this is small by

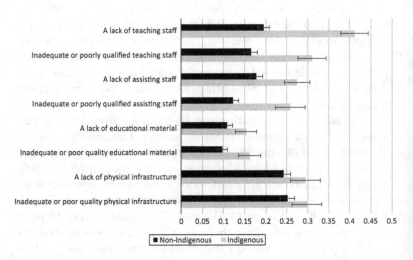

Figure 3.8 School constraints as reported by principals of Indigenous and non-Indigenous Australian students, 2015

global standards, it is slightly larger when compared with the average for non-Indigenous students of 13.2 students for every teacher. This difference was not, however, statistically significant. When I looked at a more direct measure (the average class size in the school), there was also no statistically significant difference in the probability of attending a school where the average class size was 25 students or more. In Australia at least, Indigenous students seem to experience similar student/teacher ratios to their non-Indigenous counterparts.

School capacity constraints and learning restrictions

School principals were also asked whether the capacity of the school in providing instruction was hindered by constraints in teaching staff or materials. Principals were asked about eight different issues, including shortages of teaching materials or qualified teachers. Figure 3.8 gives the proportion of Indigenous and non-Indigenous students where the school principal reported the existence of each of the constraints.

Indigenous students were significantly and substantially more likely to be attending a school where the school principal reported almost all of the capacity constraints. The only exception is for the question on 'Inadequate or poor quality physical infrastructure', where the difference is not quite statistically significant (though large in absolute terms). For the teaching questions, the differences were quite substantial. For

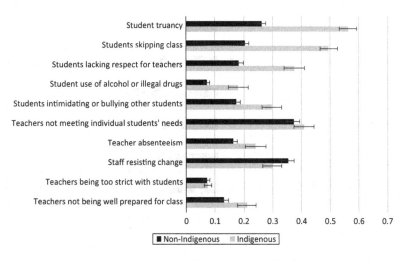

Figure 3.9 School climate as reported by principals of Indigenous and non-Indigenous Australian students, 2015

example, around 41 per cent of Indigenous students attend a school where the principal reported a lack of teaching staff compared with around 19 per cent for non-Indigenous students.

A separate set of questions were asked regarding the school climate for the students. There were ten questions in total, with Figure 3.9 once again giving the differences by Indigenous status.

There was much greater variation in the school climate questions, though in general they still showed that Indigenous students were more likely to be attending schools where the principal reported significant issues. Differences were large and statistically significant for student truancy; students skipping class; students lacking respect for teachers; student use of alcohol or illegal drugs; and students intimidating or bullying other students. There were also large gaps for teacher absenteeism and teachers not being prepared for class.

These are all very significant issues, and likely to translate into a worse schooling experience for Indigenous students. If replicated for other Indigenous populations internationally (and there is no reason to suggest it wouldn't be), the schools that Indigenous students attend are likely to be perceived to have much lower returns (and greater social costs) than those which non-Indigenous students attend. Or to put it another way, the school system would appear to be exacerbating, rather than ameliorating the external factors that inhibit school participation.

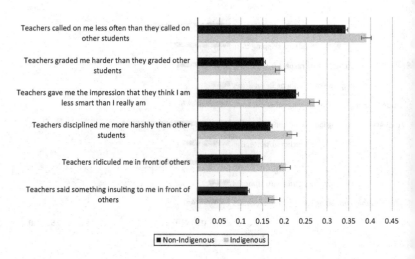

Figure 3.10 School experience as reported by Indigenous and non-Indigenous
        Australian students, 2015

Students in PISA are also asked directly about their experience at
school. Answers to these six questions tell us something about the
quality of schooling that Indigenous students (in Australia) experience,
as well as more directly what some of the social costs of school might
be. And the results are very damning (Figure 3.10).

Indigenous students are significantly and substantially more likely
to report a range of negative experiences in their schools than their
non-Indigenous counterparts. Indigenous students felt they were called
on less, graded harder, thought to be less smart than they actually are
and disciplined more harshly. These are in some ways passive forms
of unfair treatment that nonetheless are likely to have large negative
effects. However, the last two measures are even more active forms of
unfair treatment, with Indigenous students much more likely to feel that
they were ridiculed or insulted in front of others.

Relationship between school outcomes and school attendance

It would be highly surprising if these experiences did not have a negative
effect on the human capital development of Indigenous Australians.
Given the qualitative literature in other countries, we would also expect
that similar differences would be found for Indigenous peoples across a
variety of school systems. It is very difficult with cross-sectional data to

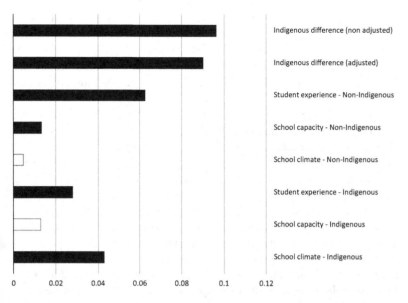

Figure 3.11 Relationship between school attendance of Indigenous and non-Indigenous Australian students and school capacity constraints, school climate and school experience, 2015

prove that such experiences have a causal impact though. It is plausible that those Indigenous students or families who have disengaged from school opt into different schools from those who are engaged. Plausible, though I must say less likely than the causality running in the opposite direction. Either way, there is a very strong negative association between school characteristics and one form of school engagement – daily school attendance.

In Figure 3.11, I present a number of summary measures of the association between school outcomes and the probability of having skipped school at least once in the previous two weeks. To simplify the analysis I use indices of school climate, school capacity and school experiences, which have been calculated from a principal components analysis of the underlying variables and scaled to have a mean of zero and a standard deviation of one.

The first bar gives the difference in probability between Indigenous and non-Indigenous students without controlling for any characteristics. It shows that an Indigenous student has a probability of skipping school at least once equal to 0.382 compared with a non-Indigenous student with a probability of 0.286 (a difference of 0.097). This is large and statistically significant. When I control (or hold constant) the difference across the three indices, there is still a large and statistically significant difference, but it is slightly smaller than when these characteristics are not controlled for (0.090 compared with 0.097). School characteristics and experiences explain some, but not all, of the differences in non-attendance between Indigenous and non-Indigenous students.

The next three bars give the association with the three indices for non-Indigenous Australians, with the last three bars giving the association for Indigenous students. The way to interpret these bars is that they are the predicted differences in the probability of skipping school from a one standard deviation increase in the index value, while holding the other two index values constant. If the bar is hollow, then that difference is not statistically significant, otherwise it is statistically significant at the 5 per cent level of significance at least (though as it turns out, they are significant at the 1 per cent level of significance as well).

Looking at the last three bars, there is no association between school capacity constraints and the probability of skipping school. This is in some ways disappointing or at least problematic as of the characteristics studied in this section, they are the ones that are most amenable to intervention at the system level. The other two indices do, however, have a significant association. If students have worse experiences (more likely to report unfair treatment from their teachers) or if their principal reports issues to do with the school climate, then an Indigenous student is much more likely to skip school.

Once again, it is not possible to make causal statements about these findings. It might be that the causality runs in the opposite direction or that there are an additional set of factors that are not captured in the model and that are correlated with the outcome as well as the explanatory variables. However, Figures 3.8–3.10 give very strong evidence that Indigenous students in Australia have substantially worse schooling circumstances than their non-Indigenous counterparts, and Figure 3.11 gives strong *prima facie* evidence that these differences are likely to predict (and probably cause) disengagement from school.

Notes

1 I include those who are serving in the armed forces as being employed, as the focus is on individual-level outcomes, rather than obtaining an estimate of the level of labour demand.

2 The model includes a linear and non-linear age variable. I predict employment and income conditional on employment for someone aged 40 years in

2016; however qualitative conclusions do not vary if I make my predictions at a different point on the age distribution or in a different year.

3 The estimation model uses a natural log dependent variable, with the predictions converted to linear income.

4 These differences are estimated for someone with a high school diploma (at aged 40, and in 2016). Once again, qualitative conclusions don't vary if differences are estimated at a different level of education.

5 http://strongersmarter.com.au/about/history/.

References

Altonji, J. G. and R. M. Blank (1999). "Race and gender in the labor market." *Handbook of Labor Economics* **3**: 3143–3259.

Barnett, W. S. (1998). "Long-term cognitive and academic effects of early childhood education on children in poverty." *Preventive Medicine* **27**(2): 204–207.

Behrendt, L., S. Larkin, R. Griew and P. Kelly (2012). *Review of higher education access and outcomes for Aboriginal and Torres Strait Islander people: Final report*. Australian Government.

Bertrand, M. and S. Mullainathan (2004). "Are Emily and Greg more employable than Lakisha and Jamal? A field experiment on labor market discrimination." *American Economic Review* **94**(4): 991–1013.

Biddle, N. (2006). "The age at which Indigenous Australians undertake qualifications: A descriptive analysis." *Australian Journal of Adult Education* **46**(2).

Biddle, N. (2013). "Comparing self perceived and observed labour market discrimination in Australia." *Economic Papers: A Journal of Applied Economics and Policy* **32**(3): 383–394.

Biddle, N., M. Howlett, B. Hunter and Y. Paradies (2013). "Labour market and other discrimination facing Indigenous Australian." *Australian Journal of Labour Economics* **16**(1): 91.

Black, S. E. and P. J. Devereux (2011). "Recent developments in intergenerational mobility." *Handbook of Labor Economics* **4**: 1487–1541.

Blanden, J. (2013). "Cross-country rankings in intergenerational mobility: A comparison of approaches from economics and sociology." *Journal of Economic Surveys* **27**(1): 38–73.

Booth, A. L., A. Leigh and E. Varganova (2012). "Does ethnic discrimination vary across minority groups? Evidence from a field experiment." *Oxford Bulletin of Economics and Statistics* **74**(4): 547–573.

Card, D. and A. B. Krueger (1992). "Does school quality matter? Returns to education and the characteristics of public schools in the United States." *Journal of Political Economy* **100**(1): 1–40.

Dale, S. B. and A. B. Krueger (2014). "Estimating the effects of college characteristics over the career using administrative earnings data." *Journal of Human Resources* **49**(2): 323–358.

Forrest, A. (2014). *The Forrest review: creating parity*. Canberra, Commonwealth of Australia.

Fryer, R. G. (2017). "The production of human capital in developed countries: Evidence from 196 randomized field experiments." *Handbook of Economic Field Experiments* **2**: 95–322.

Gray, M., B. Hunter and N. Biddle (2014). "The economic and social benefits of increasing Indigenous employment." *CAEPR Topical Issue* 1/2014.

Heckman, J. J., J. Stixrud and S. Urzua (2006). *The effects of cognitive and noncognitive abilities on labor market outcomes and social behavior*, Chicago: National Bureau of Economic Research.

Herrnstein, R. J. and C. Murray (2010). *Bell curve: Intelligence and class structure in American life*, New York: Simon and Schuster.

Hertz, T., T. Jayasundera, P. Piraino, S. Selcuk, N. Smith and A. Verashchagina (2007). "The inheritance of educational inequality: International comparisons and fifty-year trends." *The BE Journal of Economic Analysis & Policy* **7**(2).

Hull, R. and S. Edsall (2001). *No small matter: Quality preschools benefit children and society*. Melbourne, Australian Education Union.

Jackson, C. K., R. C. Johnson and C. Persico (2015). "The effects of school spending on educational and economic outcomes: Evidence from school finance reforms." *The Quarterly Journal of Economics* **131**(1): 157–218.

Kronemann, M. (1998). *Towards a national plan for preschool education*. Melbourne, Australian Education Union.

Langton, M. and Z. Ma Rhea (2009). "Indigenous education and the ladder to prosperity." *Perspectives*: 95–119.

Lareau, A. (1987). "Social class differences in family-school relationships: The importance of cultural capital." *Sociology of Education*: 73–85.

Marks, G. N. (2013). *Education, social background and cognitive functioning: The decline of the social*. London: Routledge.

Martin, K. (2012). "Aboriginal early childhood: past, present, and future". In J. P. J. Lampert (ed.), *Introductory indigenous studies in education: The importance of knowing*. Sydney: Pearson Education: 27–40.

Morgan, G. (2012). "Urban transitions: Aboriginal men, education and work in Redfern Waterloo." *Postcolonial Studies* **15**(2): 267–281.

Morphy, F. (2007). *Agency, contingency and census process: Observations of the 2006 Indigenous Enumeration Strategy in remote Aboriginal Australia*, Acton, AU: ANU E Press.

Neumark, D. (2016). *Experimental research on labor market discrimination*, National Bureau of Economic Research.

Perso, T. and C. Hayward (2015). *Teaching Indigenous students: Cultural awareness and classroom strategies for improving learning outcomes*, Crows Nest, AU: Allen & Unwin.

Piketty, T. (2014). *Capital in the twenty-first century*, Cambridge, MA: Harvard University Press.

Reeves, R., J. Venator and K. Howard (2014). *The character factor: Measures and impact of drive and prudence*. Washington, DC: Brookings Institute.

Rothman, S. (2009). "Estimating attrition bias in the year 9 cohorts of the longitudinal surveys of Australian youth: Technical report no. 48." *LSAY Technical Reports*: 48.

Sandel, M. J. (2010). *Justice: What's the right thing to do?* London: Penguin Books.

Schwab, R. G. and D. Sutherland (2001). *Building Indigenous learning communities*. Discussion Paper no. 225, Centre for Aboriginal Economic Policy Research, Canberra.

Steering Committee for the Review of Government Service Provision (SCRGSP) (2014). *Overcoming Indigenous disadvantage: Key indicators 2014.* Canberra, Productivity Commission.

Sussman, R. W. (2014). *The myth of race: The troubling persistence of an unscientific idea*, Cambridge, MA: Harvard University Press.

Part II

Programmes that help improve the human capital development of Indigenous peoples

4   Improving the schooling experience of Indigenous peoples

Having introduced the HCM and discussed some of the evidence related to participation and outcomes, the next three chapters now turn to some of the policy interventions that have been tried to support the education participation of Indigenous peoples. In Chapter 5 I look at Indigenous-specific education institutions, with Chapter 6 looking at the evidence related to financial support tied to human capital investments (specifically, conditional cash transfers, or CCTs). In this chapter, I look at a particular type of investment within the schools that both Indigenous and non-Indigenous students attend, tied to the concept of reconciliation.

This is in no way a comprehensive analysis of all the potential policy interventions that may (or may not) improve the human capital levels of Indigenous peoples, or that lead to positive development outcomes. Rather, it is a summary of three types of interventions, what the evidence says about them, and the relationship with the HCM.

Reconciliation in Australia, and in schools and early learning services

What is reconciliation?

Reconciliation is a concept that has very broad support among the Indigenous and non-Indigenous population of Australia. Although it is a number of years ago now, many people will still remember taking part in or seeing the images of the Walk for Reconciliation across Sydney Harbour Bridge in 2000. According to the National Museum of Australia,[1] 'The Bridge Walk for Reconciliation and similar events that took place around Australia in the weeks following were collectively the biggest demonstration of public support for a cause that has ever taken place in Australia' and 'The march was a public expression of support for meaningful reconciliation between Australia's Indigenous and non-Indigenous peoples.'

What we specifically mean by reconciliation, however, is much more complex. The former Prime Minister John Howard famously focused on improvements in socioeconomic status under his (and his government's) definition of Practical Reconciliation (Altman and Hunter 2003). Patrick Dodson, current Senator for the Labor Party in Western Australia, highlights the importance of recognising difference and stated in a recent ANU (where I work) Reconciliation Lecture[2] that:

> Reconciliation will come when governments stop trying to make us the same as everyone else. When they desist from constantly demanding we conform to every facet of mainstream society that wants to break down or deny who we are, especially with regard to our unique relationship to our land and community.

Professor Dodson also stated that 'Reconciliation cannot be taken for granted. It is not a feel-good word that can be bandied around lightly, or be co-opted to obscure the need for restorative justice.' This echoes a statement made by an ANU colleague Will Sanders (2002) that reconciliation 'will be a journey without end, that each generation of Indigenous and settler Australians will have to come to their own understanding of the relationship of each to the other, in both its historical and contemporary socio-economic dimensions'.

Reconciliation Australia (RA) is a non-governmental organisation in Australia focused on achieving such aims. RA states that its 'vision of reconciliation is based on five inter-related dimensions: race relations, equality and equity, unity, institutional integrity and historical acceptance'.[3] RA also argues that these dimensions are affected by wider structural and policy processes and that they are inherently inter-related, stating that 'Australia can only achieve full reconciliation if we progress in all five dimensions, weaving them together to become a whole.'

With such a complicated and in many ways disputed concept, it is always going to be a challenge if not an impossible task to design and evaluate a coherent policy response that incorporates all of the definitions and components of reconciliation that are held within the Aboriginal and Torres Strait Islander population, and the rest of Australian society. It is necessary, therefore, to focus on specific aspects or domains of reconciliation. This is the approach that has been taken by RA since its establishment in 2001. RA has supported the development of Workplace Reconciliation Access Plans (RAPs), with 650 organisations across Australia having developed a RAP since 2006. RA has also been heavily involved in supporting and highlighting Indigenous governance, arguing that strong and effective governance in Indigenous organisations will allow for greater ownership and control of the policy development and service delivery process (Garling, Hunt et al. 2013).

A more recent focus of RA has been on the way in which schools and early learning services across Australia can contribute to the reconciliation process. Narragunnawali: Reconciliation in Schools and Early Learning is a national programme designed and implemented by RA.[4] *Narragunnawali* (pronounced narra-gunna-wally) is a word from the language of the Ngunnawal people meaning alive, wellbeing, coming together and peace. The programme is designed to support all Australian schools and early learning services in developing a higher level of knowledge and pride in Aboriginal and Torres Strait Islander histories, cultures and contributions. The programme is designed to be delivered at the whole-school or early learning service level, with benefits for all students and staff, as well as for the wider community.

Reconciliation in schools and early learning services

Unlike many programmes in Indigenous education (in Australia and abroad), the primary agents of change in *Narragunnawali* are not Aboriginal and Torres Strait Islander students or their families. Rather, the focus is on teachers and early learning service workers, and through them non-Indigenous students. In the short term, increasing the confidence and ability of teachers and educators to incorporate Aboriginal and Torres Strait Islander histories, cultures, perspectives and contemporary issues into curriculum planning and teaching will make for a much richer educational experience for all students. Or, in the HCM that I have been using in this book, it may reduce the social costs of school attendance that many Indigenous Australians face, as well as increase the non-monetary benefits of schooling.

We know from data from the Reconciliation Barometer (a survey conducted by RA), as well as the National Aboriginal and Torres Strait Islander Social Survey (NATSISS), that a very substantial minority of Indigenous Australians experienced some form of discrimination or unfair treatment over a 6–12 month period (Biddle, Howlett et al. 2013). For example, according to the most recent Reconciliation Barometer, 46 per cent of Indigenous respondents reported that they had experienced at least one form of racial prejudice in the 6 months preceding the survey. Therefore, most if not all Indigenous Australians are likely to experience some form of discrimination over their lifetime. This might be in the workplace; by policy or in the criminal justice system; at university; or by the general public.

In the longer term, many of the employers, policy officers, university lecturers, etc. that Indigenous Australians will interact with (and potentially face discrimination from) are current non-Indigenous students in schools or early learning services. *Narragunnawali* has the potential to shape and modify the behaviours and attitudes that lead to such discrimination, leading to a safer and more equitable environment for the future Indigenous population.

Consultation identified that *Narragunnawali* would be most effective if targeted at teachers and educators as the key drivers of reconciliation. Reconciliation Australia aims to engage teachers through the Australian Curriculum (cross-curriculum priority of Aboriginal and Torres Strait Islander histories and cultures) and the Australian Professional Standards for Teachers (Focus area 2.4). It also aims to engage early childhood educators through the Early Years Learning Framework and the Australian Children's Education and Care Quality Authority National Quality Standards. The existing reconciliation framework of developing *relationships*, showing *respect* and seeking mutual *opportunities* will be applied in schools and early learning services through classroom teaching and learning, the school or early learning service's culture and ethos, and the links with local community through *Narragunnawali's* various components. These are outlined below.

Schools and early learning services are provided with a model for action using Reconciliation Australia's existing Reconciliation Framework (*Relationships, Respect, Opportunities*), combined with a whole-school and early learning service planning model that incorporates actions *In the Classroom* (teaching, learning, curriculum), *Around the School or early learning service* (the ethos within the gate) and *With the Community* (the links beyond the gate).

This is done through Reconciliation Action Plans (RAPs), created through an online tool (RAP developer). The RAP developer incorporates web-based project management and provides whole-school or early learning service actions that are used to build a RAP. For schools and early learning services, the online tool facilitates the development of plans to communicate with relevant local organisations and communities, and provides a suite of actions to choose from. It allows access to resources including teaching materials and links to relevant bodies and organisations.

With the introduction of the Australian Curriculum and the Early Years Learning Framework, teachers in schools and educators in early learning services, are required to engage in meaningful programming focused on Aboriginal and Torres Strait Islander histories, cultures and contributions. In response to these professional teaching requirements *Narragunnawali* promotes the use of curriculum resources which are integrated into a suite of specific RAP actions that schools and early learning services can select from within the RAP Developer to facilitate reconciliation.

The goal is to support teachers and educators to better engage with the selected RAP actions, by providing quality teaching and learning resources. These resources work to complement the professional learning strategy and, by association, teachers' and educators' engagement with their school or early learning service RAP.

The measured effects of a reconciliation in schools and early learning services programme

Narragunnawali became available to schools and early learning services in 2014, with a gradual uptake from a small number of schools and early learning services. In September 2015 there were 357 schools and early learning services that were recorded as having engaged with a RAP. On 6 April 2017, an updated version of the online platform for *Narragunnawali* was launched (Version 2.0). At that stage there were 1,230 schools and early learning services engaged, whereas by 7 November 2017, this had increased to 1,825 schools and early learning services. This is a very dramatic increase in engagement with RAPs and highlights the high level of support for *Narragunnawali* and reconciliation in general among Australian schools and early learning services. The question though, is whether this had any effects on the schools that were engaged in the programme.

Results from the School Reflection Survey

One action as part of participation in a Reconciliation Action Plan is completing and reflecting on a *whole-school or early learning service Reflection Survey* (RS). The focus of the RS is to assist RAP Working Groups[5] (RAPWGs) to reflect on the current state of reconciliation in their school or early learning service as one of the first steps in developing a RAP.

The RS looks at the three main spheres of the school or early learning service – in the classroom, around the school and with the community; the most recent version of the survey has 23 questions in total. While the survey was designed as a tool for schools and early learning services, it still has significant analytical use.

In May 2016, I was asked by RA to analyse data from initial responses to the RS. A number of key findings emerged from that initial analysis. First, there was a considerable degree of uncertainty among the Working Group (who filled out the survey) about what is happening within the school or early learning service. This is particularly the case for what is happening within the classroom. This is an important point when reflecting on such programmes and their role in the human capital development of Indigenous peoples. Often we assume that teachers and other educators have much greater oversight and control over what is going on within their school, for better or worse. The RS shows that this is not necessarily the case.

A second major finding was that there was a strong relationship between some of the key measures. For example, those schools or early learning services that display a flag were much more likely to have teachers that have completed cultural competency, proficiency or awareness training and are more likely to Acknowledge Country at events at the school or early learning service. According to Reconciliation Australia:

> An Acknowledgement of Country is an opportunity for anyone to show respect for Traditional Owners and the continuing connection of Aboriginal and Torres Strait Islander peoples to Country. It can be given by both non-Indigenous people and Aboriginal and Torres Strait Islander people.[6]

Those schools or early learning services where teachers feel knowledgeable about local Aboriginal and Torres Strait Islander histories and cultures were more likely to be involved in activities with the local Aboriginal and Torres Strait Islander community. There is strong evidence, in other words, that different aspects of reconciliation in schools and early learning services are reinforcing.

The final finding from that analysis was that there are other characteristics that predict reconciliation activities and outcomes. Teachers in independent schools were reported to be less likely to be knowledgeable on Aboriginal and Torres Strait Islander issues. They were also reported to be significantly less likely to Acknowledge Country. Schools or early learning services in relatively disadvantaged areas were less likely to display an Aboriginal and/or Torres Strait Islander flag. This may be a resourcing issue. Finally, teachers in schools or early learning services in areas with a high Indigenous usual resident population were more likely to have undertaken cultural competency, proficiency or awareness training. These initial findings pointed to areas of existing strength, as well as where things can be built on.

More powerful than a single cross-section, it is also possible to link responses to the surveys through time, at least at the school or early learning service level. The second round of surveys was conducted between 6 April and 2 October 2017. In total, there were 447 responses to the survey that could be linked. We can use this data first as a cross-section of a self-selected set of schools currently engaging with *Narragunnawali*. The data shows a very high rate of support for the principles of *Narragunnawali*, with ongoing uncertainty among the RAPWGs.

Two very important questions in the survey with regards to teacher confidence are Question 2, related to incorporation of Indigenous histories, cultures and perspectives, and Question 12 on discussion of Indigenous issues during staff meetings.[7] For the first of these questions, the majority of respondents (56.1 per cent) report that in their school or early learning service around 50 per cent or more of their teachers and educators 'regularly and confidently incorporate Aboriginal and Torres Strait Islander histories, cultures, perspectives and contemporary issues'. Furthermore, around four-fifths of respondents (79.7 per cent) report that 'Aboriginal and Torres Strait Islander histories, cultures and perspectives discussed at staff meetings' at least some of the time.

Given the effect of racism on school and later life outcomes, there is likely to be considerable interest in one of the new questions on the survey that asks, 'Does your school or early learning service have an anti-racism strategy?' It is encouraging that 54.0 per cent of respondents answered that their school or early learning service did have such a strategy. What is somewhat problematic, however, is that 28.2 per cent of respondents were unsure and unable to answer the question. One might assume that an anti-racism strategy is only of use if the majority of teachers and educators are aware of it, so the fact that there is so much uncertainty, even among this self-selected group, is cause for concern.

While there is considerable knowledge of and confidence in incorporating Indigenous issues within the school, only around a quarter of respondents (25.3 per cent) reported that in the last year 50 per cent or more of teachers and educators 'collaborated with Aboriginal and Torres Strait Islander people to prepare and deliver lessons'. Around the same proportion (26.8 per cent) reported that in the last year 'Aboriginal and Torres Strait Islander community members, businesses or organisations [were] invited to be involved in activities at your school or early learning service' often (3–4 times) or regularly (five times or more). *Narragunnawali* has the potential to do much more in facilitating interaction with the community.

As the name suggests the RS is useful for schools and early learning services to reflect on what they are doing well, what they are doing less well and where there is uncertainty. It is also useful, however, to measure change through time. Specifically, there were 264 schools and early learning services for which we had information on the results from their RS prior to the *Narragunnawali 2.0* refresh, as well as data from the most recent version. By comparing the results across those two waves, it is possible to obtain some information on how comparable outcomes are changing through time. While question ordering matters, as does the exact wording of questions (Groves, Fowler Jr et al. 2011), there are 13 questions for which it is possible to compare change through time.

A very positive finding from the analysis of this linked-through-time data is that there are very few schools or early learning services that have moved backwards in the key outcome measures. For example, of the 151 schools or early learning services that reported that they were flying the Aboriginal and/or Torres Strait Islander flag when they first filled in the RS, only 11.2 per cent did not report that they were in the second wave. One might hope this percentage would be zero, but around one-in-ten schools is a relatively small share, given the quite large percentage that don't fly the flag across the total school and early learning service sample.

More importantly, in addition to the few schools and early learning services that fall backwards, there was a very large percentage of schools and early learning services that changed from not undertaking a particular activity or being unsure in the first round of the survey to undertaking it (at least some of the time) in the second wave. Some of these changes were quite substantial.

In the linked sample, there were 129 schools or early learning services that reported that none of their 'teachers and educators regularly collaborate with Aboriginal and Torres Strait Islander people in preparing and delivering lessons' or who were unsure the first time they filled in the RS. By the second wave (post 6 April2017), however, only 32.6 per cent of these 129 schools answered none or unsure to the corresponding questions.

Similarly, there were 79 schools or early learning services that reported in the first wave of the survey that none of their staff 'have undertaken some level of Aboriginal and Torres Strait Islander cultural competency, proficiency or awareness training' or that they were unsure of how many. Of those, 64.6 per cent reported that at least some of their staff had done so in the subsequent wave.

A final important and very dramatic change through time relates to acknowledgement of country. There were 97 schools or early learning services in the longitudinal sample that in the first wave reported that they 'never Acknowledge Country at regular events' or who were unsure. Of these, only five gave a similarly negative answer in the second wave of data collection.

It is not possible to attribute causality to these findings. There are other changes within education and Australian society broadly that may be increasing collaboration with peoples, participation in cultural competency, proficiency, and awareness training, and acknowledgement of country. However, the fact that such a high proportion of schools and early learning services within the programme were becoming more likely to undertake such practices is very strong *prima facie* evidence for the effectiveness of the programme in these domains.

While not as dramatic, there were also positive changes in *Narragunnawali* schools in terms of awareness of the relevant parts of the Australian curriculum; provision for reconciliation initiatives; discussion at staff meetings; welcomes to country; participation in National Reconciliation Week/National Aboriginal and Islanders Day Observance Committee (NAIDOC) week activities; and the use of Aboriginal and Torres Strait Islander advisory groups. Putting this another way, there is very strong evidence that those schools that continue to engage with *Narragunnawali* increase the types of activities that the programme is trying to support.

Results from external datasets

The RS gives some evidence that participation in *Narragunnawali* increases the types of activities that are likely to increase the benefits and decrease the costs of school attendance. However, there is also evidence that participation in the programme directly impacts teachers. It is possible to obtain some information on this through a dataset that ostensibly has very little to do with *Narragunnawali* – the Longitudinal Study of Indigenous Children (LSIC), also known as Footprints in Time. LSIC commenced in 2008 and data is collected annually from approximately 1,500 Aboriginal and Torres Strait Islander children and their families.

Primarily quantitative data is collected about:

- the children – their physical and mental health, how they develop socially and cognitively, their place in their family and community, and significant events in their life;
- the children's families and households – their health, work, lifestyle, and family and community connectedness;

- the children's communities – facilities, services, and social and community issues; and
- services – child care, education, health and other services used by the child's family.

LSIC has two cohorts: B, children who were 6 months to 2 years old at Wave 1, and K, children who were 3.5–5 years old in Wave 1. The 11 sites used in the study were selected to cover the range of socioeconomic and community environments where Australian Indigenous children live, so is not nationally representative.

For later waves of data (including that used in this chapter), interviews are carried out with three main subjects:

- Primary carer – the parent or carer who knows the study child best. In most cases this is the child's biological mother. Research Administration Officers (RAOs) undertake an extensive interview with the primary carer of every study child, asking questions about the study child, the primary carer and the household. It is a face-to-face interview.
- Study child – the main focus of the study. Data is collected through direct assessments such as vocabulary assessments, practical exercises (Who am I, the Progressive Achievement Test-Reading and the Matrix Reasoning Test) and child height and weight. The children also answer face-to-face interview questions.
- Teachers and child care workers – complete written or online questionnaires that include their observations of the study children.

The fieldwork is conducted by Department of Social Services Research Administration Officers (RAOs) who are all Aboriginal or Torres Strait Islanders. Ideally, participants are interviewed at 12-month intervals (Australian Government 2013).

Release 8.0 is the latest publicly released version of the LSIC data available, and the one that is used for this chapter. Interviews were carried out in 2015, and the survey contains information on 756 children from the B cohort and 499 children from the K cohort. The average age for children in the B cohort at the time of interview was roughly 8 years and 1 month, whereas the average age for the K cohort at the time of interview was almost exactly 11 years.

The main question of relevance for this project was asked of 414 responding teachers across both cohorts. Among a set of other questions, teachers were asked whether the school had a Reconciliation Action Plan (dsv8_12), with possible responses of [1] Currently doing;

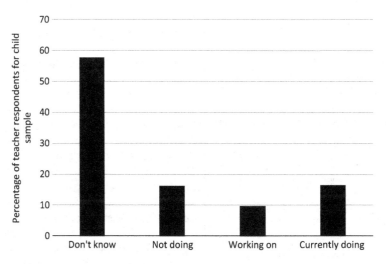

Figure 4.1 Responses to presence of Reconciliation Action Plan from the Longitudinal Study of Indigenous Children

[2] Working on; and [3] Not doing. There was also an option for 'Don't know'. The proportion of respondents in each of these categories is summarised in Figure 4.1.

Results from the LSIC show that the vast majority of teachers of Indigenous children (who were in the LSIC sample) in 2015 did not know whether their school had a RAP (57.6 per cent). Of those that did know, there was a higher percentage of teachers who were either Working on/ Currently doing a RAP (26.3 per cent) compared with those who were 'Not doing' (16.1 per cent). While it should be kept in mind that this data comes from 2015 when *Narragunnawali* was at a much earlier stage with less publicity and fewer resources available, the results from the LSIC do nonetheless show that there is a large degree of uncertainty among teachers within the schools of mid-late primary school students. If these patterns continue for later waves of the LSIC, then it would be worth considering bolstering the extent to which *Narragunnawali* provides resources, practices and advice for dissemination of knowledge within schools.

When discussing the school reflection survey, it was noted that there was significant variation in the types of activities that were being conducted within the schools and early learning services that had a RAP. By definition, this tells us very little about the extent to which those activities vary between those with and without a RAP. Figure 4.2 provides a partial answer to that question, keeping in mind that we are

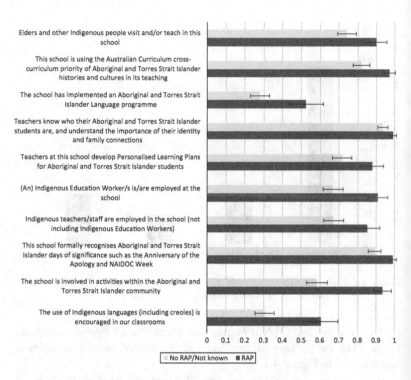

Figure 4.2 Indigenous education aspects of school by whether or not the
school has a Reconciliation Action Plan

conditioning on the sample of teachers of students from within the
LSIC. Coding the responses to a range of questions on Indigenous-
specific activities in the classroom to Yes (Working on/Doing) and
No (Don't know/Not doing), the figure gives the proportion of 'Yes'
responses by whether or not the school has a RAP (coded in a similar
way to the above).

It is very important not to assume causality from the cross-sectional
LSIC results. While it might be the case that the presence of a RAP has a
direct effect on the above outcomes, it is also possible that the causality runs
in the opposite direction. Nonetheless, the results presented in Figure 4.2
give very strong evidence that those schools with a RAP are much more
active in other aspects of Indigenous education. There is no outcome
variable for which the 'whiskers' around the estimates overlap, meaning
that all of the differences are statistically significant. Furthermore, many
of the differences are qualitatively very large. For example, schools with

a RAP (or who are working on one) are much more likely to be involved in activities within the Aboriginal and Torres Strait Islander Community than those without (including those who don't know). There is also a very large difference in encouraging the use of Indigenous languages, having an Indigenous Education Worker and implementing an Aboriginal and Torres Strait Islander Language programme.

While there is very strong evidence from the LSIC that participation in a RAP is positively correlated with a number of initiatives that are likely to benefit Indigenous children, there is very little evidence that *Narragunnawali* is having that impact yet. When parents were asked whether their child was bullied at school because they were Indigenous or whether the child looked forward to going to school each day, there was very little difference between those in a school with and without a RAP. There is some weak evidence that the proportion of Indigenous children who do not want to go to school on a given day is lower for those in a school with a RAP than those without. Specifically, 22.3 per cent of parents in non-RAP schools reported that their child did not want to go at least some of the time, compared with 16.8 per cent in RAP schools. While this difference is not statistically significant (the p-value is 0.11), it does give some support for RAP schools being a more welcoming environment for Indigenous students.

Figure 4.3 gives the proportion of students in the K cohort who responded 'Yes, always' to a series of questions about the class and the

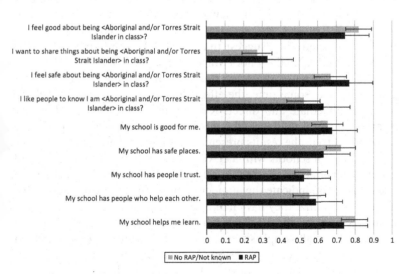

Figure 4.3 Student views on school by whether or not the school has a Reconciliation Action Plan

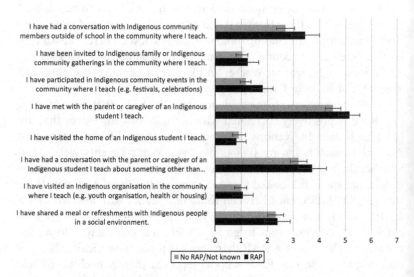

Figure 4.4 Teacher experiences by whether or not the school has a
　　　　　Reconciliation Action Plan

school. Unlike in Figure 4.2, there were no outcomes for which those children whose teacher responded that there is a RAP in the school had a significantly higher probability than those whose teachers did not (at any level of significance). This may be because the sample sizes are relatively small (between 158 and 169 students answered the questions). Nonetheless the results suggest that it will take some time before the presence of a RAP in the school will impact on the outcomes of students.

While the effect of *Narragunnawali* on Indigenous child outcomes is likely to take some time, the effect on teacher outcomes is likely to be more immediate and direct. Keeping in mind again the difficulty in making causal inference about a programme that is not part of a randomised trial, the results presented in Figure 4.4 give some evidence that teachers in schools with a RAP are much more likely to have had 'cultural experiences' than those schools without a RAP. Teachers are asked to 'Please indicate the number of times (including 0 times) in the last 6 months' that they have had a set of experiences, with Figure 4.4 giving the averages for the teachers in the RAP and no RAP schools.

Given the small sample sizes, the averages in Figure 4.4 are estimated with a fair degree of imprecision. Nonetheless, there is a significant difference in the average number of times teachers 'have participated in Indigenous community events in the community where I teach' at the

5 per cent level of significance. There is also a significant difference at the 10 per cent level of significance for two additional variables (I have had a conversation with Indigenous community members outside of school in the community where I teach; and I have met with the parent or caregiver of an Indigenous student I teach). Furthermore, there are no variables where those teachers in a non-RAP school have a higher value that is close to being statistically significant.

Schools-based programmes and the HCM

On balance, the LSIC and the RS are useful datasets that have information on schools that have a RAP and, in the case of LSIC, those that do not. The data shows that there are large differences in activities for those schools with a RAP, and those teachers in those schools are for the most part more likely to engage in positive activities within the community. There is, however, still significant uncertainty around the presence of RAPs within the schools, and there is no evidence yet that having a RAP is correlated with student outcomes. These last two areas should be monitored and evaluated as the programme matures and as schools begin to have had RAPs for much longer periods of time than was the case in 2015.

But, what can we conclude from this analysis about school-based programmes and their relationship with human capital development? Of course there are thousands of schools-based programmes across the world either focused on Indigenous peoples or likely to have some impact on them. However, there are some generalisable points.

First, there is an appetite for such programmes within the school system within Australia (and therefore potentially in other comparable countries). Since the commencement of *Narragunnawali* in 2014, the number and diversity of schools and early learning services that are engaged with the programme has increased dramatically such that by the end of 2017, nearly one out of every ten schools and early learning services in Australia have commenced or completed a RAP. This is an extraordinarily high proportion for a programme that is not compulsory and that is largely made available through an online portal that schools and early learning services need to opt into.

The programme has continued to improve and adapt since its inception. As someone involved in schools-based evaluations (including of *Narragunnawali*), this poses a number of challenges to obtain causal estimates. It is hard to know what is being evaluated! Is any positive change attributable to the first or the second iteration of the programme? Maybe there was a negative effect of the first version and a positive effect of the second, cancelling each other out in the overall evaluation. But, from a programme perspective, this demonstrates the continued investment and responsiveness to changing circumstances.

The voluntary nature of the programme is also challenging for learning about what works for Indigenous human capital development. Those schools or early learning services that opt into the programme are going to be very different in existing resources, student type and goals/aspirations from those that don't. Are differences observed between those that participate and those that do not attributable to the programme, or to pre-existing differences? I will return to this point in Chapters 5 and 6, as well as in the concluding chapter. However, it is worth raising here that knowing what works for improving the human capital of Indigenous peoples is heavily constrained by the lack of proper experimentation.

These challenges aside, the evaluation has also provided very strong evidence for the programme to be having an effect on schools, early learning services and teachers. Looking at the RS, there are very few schools and early learning services who are engaging with the programme that reduce the number of activities that they engage in through time. Even more positively, those RAP Working Groups that had reported that they were not sure or were not undertaking an activity in the initial surveys had a very high probability that they were undertaking that activity in a later follow-up. To put it another way, those schools and early learning services engaged with *Narragunnawali* maintain the activities that they are already doing and increase the activities through time.

There is even strong evidence for the positive effects of *Narragunnawali* from the Longitudinal Study of Indigenous Children (LSIC). Those teachers of Indigenous students who are in schools with a RAP are much more likely to feel that their school is engaging in a range of positive activities than those teachers in other schools. The teachers themselves are also more likely to be engaging in a range of positive activities.

The analysis has, however, identified two areas of potential focus as *Narragunnawali* continues to expand and mature. The first of these is the lack of knowledge within schools and early learning services of teachers about whether their school does or does not have a RAP, as well as knowledge about the types of activities that are undertaken. Teachers and educators obviously have very busy schedules with lesson preparation, assessment and activities outside of the classroom. However, it is vitally important that all teachers and educators are aware of what is going on with regard to reconciliation within their school or early learning service. This is a point that is likely to hold for other school-based interventions.

The second caveat on the otherwise very positive discussion is that there is limited evidence so far that there is any effect of the programme on Indigenous children themselves. This is in many ways not surprising. Change in the measures analysed is likely to take significant time. And, the target of the policy is as much non-Indigenous students as Indigenous students. However, as the programme and evaluation continues, it will be important to continue to monitor more closely the effect on students while they are in the school or early learning service and once they have left.

Notes

1 www.nma.gov.au/online_features/defining_moments/featured/walk-for-reconciliation.
2 https://reporter.anu.edu.au/road-reconciliation.
3 www.reconciliation.org.au/about.
4 www.reconciliation.org.au/narragunnawali.
5 The RAPWG is responsible for setting up and leading the RAP and ensuring that it becomes part of the school and early learning service culture. It must include:

- people from the local Aboriginal and/or Torres Strait Islander community;
- principal/director or executive-level membership or support;
- teachers and educators;
- parent and wider community representatives.

6 www.reconciliation.org.au/wp-content/uploads/2017/11/Welcome-to-and-Acknowledgement-of-Country.pdf.
7 The specific wording for Question 2 is 'How many teachers and educators regularly and confidently incorporate Aboriginal and Torres Strait Islander histories, cultures, perspectives and contemporary issues into curriculum planning and teaching?' whereas the specific wording for Question 12 is 'How often in the last term (approximately 10 weeks) were Aboriginal and Torres Strait Islander histories, cultures and perspectives discussed at staff meetings?'

References

Altman, J. C. and B. Hunter (2003). *Monitoring 'practical' reconciliation: Evidence from the reconciliation decade, 1991–2001*. Discussion paper no. 254. Canberra, Centre for Aboriginal Economic Policy Research.

Australian Government Department of Families, Housing, Community Services and Indigenous Affairs (2013). *Footprints in time: The longitudinal study of indigenous children. Key summary report from wave 4*. www.dss.gov.au/sites/default/files/documents/08_2014/footprints_in_time_wave4.pdf

Biddle, N., M. Howlett, B. Hunter and Y. Paradies (2013). "Labour market and other discrimination facing Indigenous Australians." *Australian Journal of Labour Economics* **16**(1): 91.

Garling, S., J. Hunt, D. Smith and W. Sanders (2013). *Contested governance: Culture, power and institutions in Indigenous Australia*, Acton, AU: ANU Press.

Groves, R. M., F. J. Fowler Jr, M. P. Couper, J. M. Lepkowski, E. Singer and R. Tourangeau (2011). *Survey methodology*, New Jersey: John Wiley & Sons.

Sanders, W. (2002). *Journey without end: Reconciliation between Australia's Indigenous and settler peoples*. Discussion paper no. 237. Canberra, Centre for Aboriginal Economic Policy Research.

5 Indigenous-specific education institutions

Chapter 4 discussed one specific programme (in Australia) that aims in part to improve the schooling experience of Indigenous children and youth across the school system. A secondary (or maybe even primary) benefit of the programme is the flow-on effects to non-Indigenous children through increasing their exposure to Indigenous language, culture and community. A more intensive version of this is schools that are administered for and by the Indigenous community. As outlined in Carney (2017), there has been a long history of educational institutions designed specifically for Indigenous peoples. The experiences of Indigenous peoples in these institutions have not always been positive, with many institutions through history seeing one of their roles as encouraging or mandating assimilation into the wider non-Indigenous society. More recently though, a number of tribally controlled colleges and schools have been set up that celebrate and support Indigenous language and culture.

There is a long, negative history of non-Indigenous run schools that are targeted towards Indigenous peoples. This includes, for example, residential schools in North America that were said at the time to 'kill the Indian, save the man' (Grant 1996; Churchill 2004). While there may have been a number of policy makers and administrators of these schools that had positive intentions towards the children and youth that attended them, the evidence overwhelmingly suggests that they had negative consequences on the wellbeing of those students (Rosalyn 1991; Barnes, Josefowitz et al. 2006).

Perhaps the most rigorous causal analysis of residential schools was provided by Feir (2016). The author exploited exogenous variation in times of school opening, times of school closing, distance to schools and national policy changes. The author concludes, somewhat controversially, that there were economic benefits, alongside cultural costs. Or, as the author puts it, 'on average, residential schools achieved their goals of economic and cultural assimilation.'

Some of the reasons why residential schools had the negative effects that they appear to have had are that they weren't designed by the community of the students that attended, that children were in many cases forced to attend, and that the curriculum did not take into account the needs and aspirations of the students and their families. More recent iterations of education institutions specifically for Indigenous populations do not appear to suffer from these flaws, and it is worth reflecting on them with the HCM in mind.

One form of Indigenous-specific school that does appear to be viewed positively among many Indigenous families is the Māori boarding school system. Because the Māori population makes up a sizable share of the New Zealand/Aotearoa population, it is possible to exploit economies of scale and provide Māori language instruction and Māori-specific curriculum in both a boarding-school and day-school context. While experiences haven't been universally positive (including historically), Rogers (2017) was able to use an innovative, Indigenous research method to show that 'students described boarding school as growing their knowledge of Māori culture and language', in ways that the comparative Australian schools (that were not Indigenous run, or led) were not able to do.

An even larger set of institutions are the Tribal Colleges and Universities (TUCs) that are growing in size and scope in the US and Canada. According to Brown (2003), TUCs are defined as institutions of higher education that have been formally sanctioned by one or more tribes. Ideally, tribal colleges combine the preservation of tribal history, culture and traditions with academic preparation, vocational training and basic adult education. They tend to be located on or near Native American/First Nations reservations and provide a range of educational experiences (degree-granting and vocational education) to the Indigenous community in the area, as well as quite often the non-Indigenous community.

With such a large number of institutions across a diverse range of geographies and with a diverse set of economic resources (there were 41 listed online in the United States and 24 in Canada),[1] it is not possible to generalise their approach, or the experiences of the Indigenous students who attend. However, they all share the main characteristic of being run by and for Indigenous students (though not always exclusively so). A number of findings emerge from the literature.

Pavel, Inglebret et al. (2001) argue that TUCs 'have dramatically changed the higher education realm for American Indians and Alaska Natives' and 'are promoting a new mindset that is leading to renewed economic, social, political, cultural, and spiritual vitality through education.' Guardia and Evans (2008) state that 'By providing access, exposure to native culture, personal support, preparation for further education, and a sense of empowerment, tribal colleges are influential in advancing self-awareness, interpersonal sensitivity, intellectual development, acculturation, and identity development of their enrolled students.'

In a set of interviews with students of Tribal Colleges in the US, Black (2013) found a number of self-reported positive effects, and it is worth quoting at length:

> Overwhelmingly, students were very positive about their educational experiences; strengths included faculty and staff interactions, language and cultural preservation, and the feeling of belonging and excitement for learning. Areas for improvement included childcare, electronic support and transportation. Students felt that their education was pivotal in their success at communicating with members of their families and communities who were literate in the language and were the keepers of the tradition. They also described their education as being life-changing; they began to view education in a different perspective. They began to recruit their siblings, cousins and other family members to return to school for a GED and then to a TCU for formal education. Students also discussed the fact that they began to expect their children to attend a college or university.

Unfortunately, despite the growth in scale and diversity, there are no causal evaluations that I am aware of that compares the experience of an average Indigenous student in a TCU with an otherwise identical student in a different form of higher education. This could be through random allocation, or through exploiting other forms of exogenous variation in participation.

Ambler (2005) makes the point that 'Tribal college administrators care not only about what happens to the student but also about how the community is transformed by their graduates' and that students 'expect something more from their tribal colleges than they would from a mainstream college.' This is clearly a rationale for those institutions, but also means that those Indigenous students who decide to attend a TCU are likely to be different in many important ways from those who attend other forms of education. Indeed, Pascarella (2006) has argued that one of ten areas of important future research is to 'Extend and Expand Inquiry on Previously Ignored Students and Institutions' and 'that future inquiry might uncover unique impacts attributable to other virtually ignored institutions such as tribal colleges.'

In my view it is important to address this lack of causal evaluation and, importantly, to undertake evaluations that test what aspects of TCUs lead to success in a cost-effective manner and which ones do not.

Nonetheless, the evidence that we do have on TCUs suggests that they mitigate some of the costs of education identified previously from the HCM. Specifically, they are usually on or close to Native American reservations, making it easier for Indigenous populations in those areas to attend them without travel or moving costs (though it should be pointed out that this is not always relevant for urban Indigenous populations, which make up the majority of most Indigenous populations (Peters and Andersen 2013)). Second, by incorporating a much greater focus on Indigenous-specific instruction and material, as well as having a much greater student body that identifies as being Indigenous, the social costs are likely to be lower.

One final point to make on Indigenous-specific education is that, in addition to formal education settings controlled by Indigenous communities, there is much education (or learning) that takes place outside of any formal institution. For example, Kral and Schwab (2013) have attempted to dispel the myth that remote Indigenous communities (primarily in Australia, but also elsewhere) are universally dysfunctional with no learning or intergenerational transfer of knowledge taking place. Rather, they argue that 'Indigenous young people we met and who shared with us their insights and experiences were quietly yet deeply involved in a range of meaningful and productive learning activities in their home communities.' Unfortunately though, this learning was (in the author's view) ignored or discounted by government and those that evaluate the effectiveness of interventions.

There will continue to be many Indigenous peoples who have a preference for and see the benefit of education in formal, mainstream settings. And, the TCUs model and the successes of some Māori or other Indigenous boarding schools could and should be incorporated into as many mainstream institutions as possible. However, there is also a sizable proportion of Indigenous students who desire forms of informal learning or formal Indigenous-specific institutions, either as a complement to, or supplement for other institutions.

Note

1 This is probably an under-estimate; https://en.wikipedia.org/wiki/List_of_tribal_colleges_and_universities.

References

Ambler, M. (2005). "Tribal colleges redefining success." *Tribal College* **16**(3): 8.
Barnes, R., N. Josefowitz and E. Cole (2006). "Residential schools: Impact on Aboriginal students' academic and cognitive development." *Canadian Journal of School Psychology* **21**(1–2): 18–32.

Black, V. (2013). *Tribal colleges and universities*, PhD dissertation, Athens, GA: University of Georgia.

Brown, D. (2003). "Tribal colleges: Playing a key role in the transition from secondary to postsecondary education for American Indian students." *Journal of American Indian Education* **42**(1): 36–45.

Carney, C. (2017). *Native American higher education in the United States*, Routledge.

Churchill, W. (2004). *Kill the Indian, save the man: The genocidal impact of American Indian residential schools*, San Francisco: City Lights Books.

Feir, D. L. (2016). "The long-term effects of forcible assimilation policy: The case of Indian boarding schools." *Canadian Journal of Economics/Revue canadienne d'economique* **49**(2): 433–480.

Grant, A. (1996). *No end of grief: Indian residential schools in Canada*, ERIC.

Guardia, J. R. and N. Evans (2008). "Student development in tribal colleges and universities." *NASPA Journal* **45**(2): 237–264.

Kral, I. and R. G. Schwab (2013). *Learning spaces: Youth, literacy and new media in remote Indigenous Australia*, Acton, AU: ANU Press.

Pascarella, E. T. (2006). "How college affects students: Ten directions for future research." *Journal of College Student Development* **47**(5): 508–520.

Pavel, D. M., E. Inglebret and S. R. Banks (2001). "Tribal colleges and universities in an era of dynamic development." *Peabody Journal of Education* **76**(1): 50–72.

Peters, E. J. and C. Andersen (2013). *Indigenous in the city: contemporary identities and cultural innovation*, British Columbia, CA: UBC Press.

Rogers, J. (2017). "Photoyarn: Aboriginal and Maori girls' researching contemporary boarding school experiences." *Australian Aboriginal Studies* (1): 3.

Rosalyn, N. (1991). "The effects of residential schools on native child-rearing practices." *Canadian Journal of Native Education* **18**: 65–118.

6 Programmes that affect Indigenous peoples indirectly

Conditional cash transfers and Indigenous peoples in Latin America

Indigenous-specific programmes (including those discussed in the previous chapters) have the potential to have a significant impact on the human capital development of the targeted Indigenous populations. While the causal evidence on this is relatively light (though it should be emphasised that there is no causal evidence to the contrary), it is also quite likely that programmes driven and supported by the relevant Indigenous community have particularly strong impacts, particularly on some of the non-economic benefits of education.

There are also likely to be benefits of programmes that are not targeted towards a particular Indigenous population, but have a large number of Indigenous participants due to geography or socio-economic targeting. For example, in Australia in 2012 the former Labor Government introduced what they called the National Disability Insurance Scheme, or NDIS, in a few pilot areas, rolling the programme out nationally in 2016 (under the subsequent Coalition Government). This programme provides targeted support for Australians with a severe disability, allowing them and their carers to have greater autonomy over the types of services that they receive and the way in which they receive them. Although the NDIS was not targeted towards Indigenous Australians, there is very strong evidence that Indigenous Australians have a higher rate of disability than their non-Indigenous counterparts and have experienced a relatively poor level of support historically (Biddle, Al-Yaman et al. 2014). The NDIS therefore has the potential to have a disproportionate effect on the Indigenous population, and hopefully a positive one.

The example of the NDIS highlights that much of the investment in human capital for Indigenous peoples needs to happen outside of the school yard, or the university quad. One form of policy intervention that has been applied extensively in Latin America over the last few years (and increasingly in other parts of the world) is conditional cash transfers, or CCTs.[1] These programmes have been implemented in a number of settings around the globe in an attempt to address issues of poverty and development. Commencing in Latin America, their usage has spread through parts of Africa, Asia and the United States of America. In essence CCTs involve a transfer of cash to identified households if they commit to investments in the human capital of their children. Some programmes may include transfer of food in lieu of cash, such as the Bangladesh Food for Education programme (Ahmed and Del Ninno 2002). Common health and nutrition conditions imposed include periodic checkups, growth monitoring, vaccinations, prenatal care and attendance by mothers at periodic health information talks. In terms of education minimum attendance rates are often expected, with some programmes including performance measures as well.

In the short term, CCTs provide households from relatively disadvantaged background with a minimum consumption floor. The transfer amount can often represent a significant portion of household income, and financial hardships experienced by the recipient families can be alleviated quite rapidly. In the long term, the intended effect of these programmes is to encourage investments in human capital at the household level, with all the potential benefits discussed previously.

Arguments for and against CCTs

The inclusion of conditions in the schemes rather than simply transferring cash to families is a deliberate tactic. The transfers are targeted towards parents that are believed to under-invest in the human capital of their children. This could occur for a range of reasons including a lack of information, conflicts of interest within the household with regard to how to utilise resources and incomplete altruism, where parental decisions are not fully consistent with what the child would have chosen if able to make such a decision. The attached conditions that need to be met are believed to ensure that parents undertake these investments (Fiszbein and Schady 2009).

There are ongoing debates in the development literature around the efficacy and ethics of CCTs (Freeland 2007). The transfer of payments of welfare upon satisfaction of conditions draws in part upon the philosophy of mutual obligations in order to modify behaviour. The idea underpinning this is that social and moral norms and values should be required of those receiving welfare payments. Payments are provided to promote activities which will advance social freedoms (Yeatman 2000). Emphasis is on self-reliance and the idea that paying individuals to increase their human capital will be beneficial for themselves as well as the state.

This philosophy has been framed as a "new paternalism" where the government is seen to have an active role in re-shaping the behaviour of welfare recipients (Mead 1997). Paternalistic incentives are framed as securing the interests of individuals, even if they contradict their freedom in the short term. For instance, interventions could circumvent the individual's choice to partake in risky behaviour such as leaving school prematurely without marketable skills.

There is indeed a significant divergence in the level of conditions attached to the different programmes in operation, as well as in views on the extent to which these conditions actually matter. Some CCTs have quite minimal conditions and monitoring in place. In the Bono de Desarrollo Humano programme in Ecuador for instance, school participation is not monitored and penalties are not enforced.

Baird, Ferreira et al. (2013) found that both CCTs and unconditional cash transfers improved the odds of children being at school (41 per cent and 23 per cent respectively, with a statistically insignificant p-value of 0.183). However, when intensity of conditions was the only independent variable, differences were more statistically significant. Each unit increase in the intensity of conditionality was accompanied by an increase of 7 per cent in the odds of enrolment. These results are consistent with experiments performed in Malawi and Burkina Faso where all cash transfers led to increases in school enrolment whether or not conditions were in place. The inclusion of conditions, however, caused further increases in impacts on both programmes.

Counter to the above, a study of a programme delivered by the Moroccan Government found that a ' "labelled' cash transfer produced a greater impact on attendance rates than one with formal conditions attached. The labelled transfer was packaged as an educational endorsement from the Ministry of Education and was administered by school headmasters, but no formal conditions such as attendance rates were imposed. Benhassine, Devoto et al. (2015) attribute this to an endorsement effect. Families were positively influenced about the value of education as a result of the programme and subsequently sought to make investments in their children's schooling.

Apart from the addition of conditions, there are several other aspects that distinguish CCTs from other means of welfare payments. These programmes are implemented with explicit acknowledgment that households and families are central to the cycle of intergenerational poverty. Strategic interventions at this level are therefore necessary to end the cycle. The interventions contained within CCTs are also targeted at key points in the life cycle. Measures are ordinarily aimed towards improving maternal health and nutrition, under-five health, and the transition from primary to secondary school (Valencia Lomelí 2008). Arguably, these are stages where assistance to recipients would be most necessary and effective.

Most programmes also are geared towards mothers as the recipients of payments. This is predicated on the view that mothers are the key decision makers in terms of the health and education of their family. This has been argued to empower women through strengthening their participation in the household as well as raising their self-esteem. However, some have argued (Gaarder, Glassman et al. 2010) that this may also reinforce a traditional division of labour, with the transfers confirming that domestic duties are the domain of women, and difficulties may also arise in family structures that do not follow Western norms.

The measured effect of CCTs

CCTs are generally considered to be successful in achieving increased rates of school enrolment and attendance. Practically every implemented programme has demonstrated positive results in terms of enrolment and attendance. Where the programmes have been concerned with the transitional rates to secondary school, these too have been improved. Additionally, positive effects have been demonstrated in reducing drop-out rates. Generally, the impacts of the CCT on enrolment are larger in countries where enrolment rates are originally low (Fiszbein, Schady et al. 2009).

Spill-over effects have also been evident. School enrolments in Mexico for Progresa rose even among children from families who were above the cut-off rate for receiving the transfers, arguably due to a peer effect (Bobonis and Finan 2002). Peers were found to have considerable influence on enrolment decisions, especially among children from relatively poorer households.

The results that CCTs produce in terms of actual learning outcomes are less clear. Quality of education is rarely implemented into programme evaluation design. Additionally, evaluating final outcomes in education is not necessarily straightforward. Simply comparing the test results of children in CCT 'treatment' and 'control' groups would not necessarily lead to accurate estimates. Additionally, many of the programmes are relatively recent and long-term evaluations of outcomes have not been performed.

Assessments of CCT impacts on outcomes have been conducted for Progresa (Behrman, Sengupta et al. 2000) and the BDH programme in Ecuador (Ponce and Bedi 2010). Neither evaluation found a significant effect of the CCT on test scores. Behrman, Parker et al. (2005) also assessed the performance on Woodcock-Johnson tests based on the length of time involved in the Oportunidades programme. They found that students that participated in the programme for an additional two years did not perform better on the tests than the children who had been involved for a relatively shorter period of time.

Positive long-term effects have been observed from the Nicaraguan RPS programme. Barham, Macours et al. (2012) surveyed male students who had participated in the programme ten years after they ceased receiving payments. The participants in this study had begun participating in the programme in 2000 and received payments for three years. As part of the RPS programme, they were interviewed prior to commencement. Between November 2009 and 2011, data was collected on the households. A sample of households was also taken that had children of ages critical to the long-term evaluation. This study focused on the male cohort aged between 9 and 12 in 2000. By the time the follow-up was conducted, the vast majority of these had left school and were engaged in economic or domestic activities.

Not only might the conditional aspects of CCTs not be necessary, but the imposition of conditions may have direct negative consequences. Some households may find it too costly to comply with conditions. This may be the case if services are too inaccessible, or if the opportunity costs of studying are too high. Programmes may also impose distortions on the behaviour of families. Parents may be forced to send their children to bad schools or clinics. Children may also miss out on learning valuable lifestyle and household skills though sacrificing time to participate in schooling.

There is also an argument that CCTs displace labour market participation among the adults in the programme. If people are receiving a payment tied to their child's participation in human capital development, but not tied to their own labour market participation, then there is a fear that this will discourage people from working. This is not too different from the argument made against 'passive welfare' or welfare dependency, most prominently by Noel Pearson (2000), who has argued that income support if not tied to productive activity will lead to a lack of incentives for Indigenous people in many communities to make the types of changes to their behaviour that will lead to long-term improvements for themselves, their children and their community. According to Pearson (2000), writing with regard to Cape York in northern Australia, 'Most economic activity, including the operation of community enterprises, occurs within the passive welfare economy, and is reliant upon government transfers.'

This form of economic activity, he believes, is particularly problematic for the following three reasons. According to Pearson (2000) again, passive welfare is 'an irrational economic relationship' as there are no obligations placed on the recipient, it is a 'method of governmental action' in that a superior power has all the rights and responsibilities, and it is 'a mentality' which is 'internalised and perpetuated by recipients who see themselves as victimised or incapable.'

Leaving aside the specifics of the relationship between welfare receipt and Indigenous peoples in Australia, a recent review article by Banerjee, Hanna et al. (2017) looked at the negative employment effects of CCTs. They start off by stating that 'policy-makers are often concerned about whether transfer programmes of this type [CCTs] discourage work.' They analyse this question by pooling 'the results of seven randomized controlled trials of government run cash transfer programs from six countries worldwide to examine the program impacts on labor supply.' According to the authors:

> Reanalyzing the data allows us to make comparisons that are as comparable as possible, using harmonized data definitions and empirical strategies. Reanalyzing the micro data directly also allows us to pool effects across studies to yield tighter bounds than would be possible from any single study.

The results are fairly compelling. Specifically, Banerjee, Hanna et al. (2017) find that 'Across the seven programmes, we find no observable impacts of the cash transfer programs on either the propensity to work or the overall number of hours worked, for either men or women.'

Differences in outcomes of CCTs between Indigenous and non-Indigenous households

It should never be assumed that because a programme has been demonstrated to have a positive effect on the total population (or to not have any negative effects) that these results would hold for population groups within that country. Known in the evaluation literature as heterogeneous treatment effects (Xie, Brand et al. 2012; Glennerster and Takavarasha 2013), this is particularly the case for Indigenous peoples who have had a very different historical experience with the State, and often very different economic circumstances, cultural values, preferences and exposure to wider societal influences.

In the case of CCTs, however, there have been positive results demonstrated in the outcomes of Indigenous households specifically. Most of these evaluations, however, have been based on the Progresa/

Oportunidades programme in Mexico. Bando and Lopez-Calva (2006) used data from the programme to look at the interaction between health and Indigenous status of the household. They monitored changes in behaviour over a three year period. Comparisons were made between Indigenous and non-Indigenous children from both a control and a treatment group who did not participate in the programme. Participating Indigenous children demonstrated higher rates of health monitoring visits than those not in the programme. Out of the four groups, the incidence of morbidity among 0–2–year-olds declined most rapidly. Additionally, negative rates of illness were demonstrated compared with non-Indigenous, non-participating children, indicating a positive impact on health.

Bando, Patrinos et al. (2005) also found positive impacts of Progresa on Indigenous children in paid work. Before the implementation of the programme, Indigenous children had a greater probability of working rather than attending school in comparison with non-Indigenous children. However, after exposure to the programme, this was reversed. Consideration, however, was given to the fact that the child labour force is greater in Indigenous areas, particularly in rural settings.

More recently, Lopez-Calva and Patrinos (2015) undertook a review of the impact of Progresa on a range of outcomes of Indigenous children in Mexico, looking separately at children who speak an Indigenous language only compared with those who speak Spanish and an Indigenous language. Using an extensive range of data and robust methods, it is worth quoting the findings at length. Specifically, the authors find that:

> While indigenous children had a greater probability of working before the intervention, this probability is reversed after treatment in the program. Indigenous monolingual children also had lower school attainment compared with Spanish-speaking or indigenous bilingual children. After the program, school attainment among indigenous children increased, reducing the gap. In terms of child labor, the larger reduction is in the group of bilingual children... These results are consistent with findings in other papers related to indigenous schooling barriers ... whereby monolingual indigenous children have a higher hurdle to overcome when compared with those who are bilingual.

Returning to the discussion in the introduction to this book, the HCM would predict such findings, as CCTs reduce the costs of human capital investments (direct and opportunity). It is also worth reflecting on the outcomes used in Lopez-Calva and Patrinos (2015) and other evaluations of CCTs or other programmes for Indigenous children specifically. My long-term reading of the literature on Indigenous development and wellbeing would suggest to me that there would be very few Indigenous leaders who wouldn't value reductions in child labour and improvements in schooling outcomes and health. To the extent that CCTs or similar programmes lead to these outcomes, it is worth trialling and evaluating across a much greater range of Indigenous communities.

Despite the importance of such measures to the Indigenous population, they are also incomplete. Given the importance of Indigenous languages and cultural production to Indigenous peoples, it would be important to test the impact of such programmes on such Indigenous-specific measures. The research evidence would also suggest that the positive incentives embedded within CCTs are more effective than the punitive approach used in income management programmes in Australia (Bray, Gray et al. 2014).

A final point that I will return to in the concluding chapters is the standard of evidence used to evaluate CCTs. By using careful (and ethical) random assignment of exposure to the programme, it is possible to set up a rigorous counterfactual and compare a child (Indigenous or otherwise) who has been exposed to the programme with an otherwise equivalent Indigenous child who has not. Any differences in outcomes can then be attributed to the programme, rather than some other unobserved characteristics. While such approaches cannot automatically be applied to the Indigenous context, in the absence of such approaches it is next to impossible to measure whether a programme has had any effect on outcomes.

Note

1 A significant proportion of the background research for this section was undertaken by Aleesha Nathan, when she was an Aurora intern at the ANU Centre for Aboriginal Economic Policy Research. This research assistance was greatly appreciated.

References

Ahmed, A. U. and C. Del Ninno (2002). "The Food for Education program in Bangladesh: An evaluation of its impact on educational attainment and food security." *Food Consumption and Nutrition Division Discussion Paper* **138**.

Baird, S., F. H. Ferreira, B. Özler and M. Woolcock (2013). "Relative effectiveness of conditional and unconditional cash transfers for schooling outcomes in developing countries: a systematic review." *Campbell Systematic Reviews* **9**(8).

Bando, R. and L. Lopez-Calva (2006). *Conditional cash transfers and indigenous people's health: Is there a differential impact of Progresa between indigenous and non-indigenous households?* Working Paper, Tecnológico de Monterrey, Campus Ciudad de México.

Bando, R., H. A. Patrinos, R. Bando and L. F. López-Calva (2005). *Child labor, school attendance, and indigenous households: evidence from Mexico.* World Bank Publications.

Banerjee, A. V., R. Hanna, G. E. Kreindler and B. A. Olken (2017). "Debunking the stereotype of the lazy welfare recipient: Evidence from cash transfer programs." *The World Bank Research Observer* 32(2): 155–184.

Barham, T., K. Macours and J. A. Maluccio (2012). "More schooling and more learning? Effects of a 3-year conditional cash transfer program in Nicaragua after 10 years." www.aeaweb.org/conference/2013/retrieve.php?pdfid=216.

Behrman, J. R., S. W. Parker and P. E. Todd (2005). *Long-term impacts of the Oportunidades conditional cash transfer program on rural youth in Mexico,* Discussion papers, Ibero America Institute for Economic Research.

Behrman, J. R., P. Sengupta and P. Todd (2000). *"The impact of PROGRESA on achievement test scores in the first year."* Washington DC: International Food Policy Research Institute.

Benhassine, N., F. Devoto, E. Duflo, P. Dupas and V. Pouliquen (2015). "Turning a shove into a nudge? A 'labeled cash transfer' for education." *American Economic Journal: Economic Policy* 7(3): 86–125.

Biddle, N., F. Al-Yaman, M. Gourley, M. Gray, J. Bray, B. Brady, L. Pham, E. Williams and M. Montaigne (2014). *Indigenous Australians and the National Disability Insurance Scheme,* Acton, AU: ANU Press.

Bobonis, G. and F. Finan (2002). "Transfers to the poor increase the schooling of the non-poor: The case of Mexico's Progresa program." University of California at Berkeley. https://pdfs.semanticscholar.org/ff58/512bf07c006a1 2bdb5c3b63a7b044cebbde5.pdf

Bray, J. R., M. Gray, K. Hand and I. Katz (2014). *Evaluating new income management in the Northern Territory: Final evaluation report.* Sydney: Social Policy Research Centre.

Fiszbein, A., N. R. Schady and F. H. Ferreira (2009). *Conditional cash transfers: reducing present and future poverty,* World Bank Publications.

Freeland, N. (2007). "Superfluous, pernicious, atrocious and abominable? The case against conditional cash transfers." *IDS Bulletin* 38(3): 75–78.

Gaarder, M. M., A. Glassman and J. E. Todd (2010). "Conditional cash transfers and health: Unpacking the causal chain." *Journal of Development Effectiveness* 2(1): 6–50.

Glennerster, R. and K. Takavarasha (2013). *Running randomized evaluations: A practical guide.* Princeton, NJ: Princeton University Press.

Lopez-Calva, L. F. and H. A. Patrinos (2015). "Exploring the differential impact of public interventions on indigenous people: Lessons from Mexico's conditional cash transfer program." *Journal of Human Development and Capabilities* 16(3): 452–467.

Mead, L. M. (1997). "The rise of paternalism." In L. M. Mead (ed.), *The new paternalism: Supervisory approaches to poverty*. Brookings Institution Press: 1–38.

Pearson, N. (2000). "Passive welfare and the destruction of Indigenous society in Australia." In P. Saunders (ed.), *Reforming the Australian welfare state*, Melbourne: Australian Institute of Family Studies. 136–155.

Ponce, J. and A. S. Bedi (2010). "The impact of a cash transfer program on cognitive achievement: The Bono de Desarrollo Humano of Ecuador." *Economics of Education Review* **29**(1): 116–125.

Valencia Lomelí, E. (2008). "Conditional cash transfers as social policy in Latin America: An assessment of their contributions and limitations." *Annual Review of Sociology* **34**: 475–499.

Xie, Y., J. E. Brand and B. Jann (2012). "Estimating heterogeneous treatment effects with observational data." *Sociological Methodology* **42**(1): 314–347.

Yeatman, A. (2000). "Mutual obligation: What kind of contract is this?" In P. Saunders (ed.), *Reforming the welfare state*. Melbourne: Australian Institute of Health and Welfare. 156–177.

Part III

Using the Human Capital Model to improve the outcomes of Indigenous peoples

7 Education for all

Using the Human Capital Model for education equity in the twenty-first century

Low levels of education participation and completion underpin a number of poor outcomes for Indigenous peoples across the developing and developed world. This includes low life expectancy, high morbidity across a number of highly treatable conditions, low levels of engagement with the labour market and high rates of poverty and deprivation. Indigenous peoples in many parts of the world are less likely to have completed high school or have a post-school qualification; less likely to be participating in education while in their childhood, youth or adolescence; more likely to be absent from school on a given day; and in the case of Australia where this data is most easily available, less likely to meet national benchmarks for literacy and numeracy.

These findings aren't inevitable. There are many Indigenous peoples who have engaged with formal education highly successfully, and used this to change the societies in which they live (as well as those institutions themselves). And, there are many education institutions that have found a way to support this. Furthermore, in some countries and many regions within countries, there has been a catch-up in many forms of education participation and attainment between Indigenous peoples and their non-Indigenous counterparts.

Despite these positive trajectories though, a large gap in education still remains. Furthermore, while Indigenous peoples in many countries are catching up in terms of high school completion and engagement with post-school education, the bar is continually being raised in terms of the credentials required for particular occupations and positions within the income distribution. Education is in many ways a positional good (Hollis 1982; Adnett and Davies 2002; Van de Werfhorst 2011) which means that if I have a high school diploma, but you have a Bachelor degree, you are going to get the job even if I am perfectly qualified and have the skills for that position. Even more problematically from a measurement and a social justice point of view, if my Bachelor degree is from a local college that still provides a wonderful set of training, but yours is from an exclusive Ivy League institution, you will most likely get the job ahead of me.

On the one hand, much of the observed differences in education participation in developed countries at least are driven by decisions made by the parents of Indigenous children, and by those children themselves as they reach youth and adulthood. For almost all Indigenous peoples in Australia, Canada, New Zealand and the US, there is a primary school and usually a secondary school/tertiary education institution available near where they live. And, unlike in the past, there are no legal barriers to education participation. For many Indigenous peoples in low or middle income countries, the standard and availability of education is improving. But, and this is one of the key points from the discussion in this book and from the Human Capital Model (HCM) broadly, these decisions are being made under very different circumstances from those under which non-Indigenous children and their families make such decisions.

The HCM is a very simple, but in my view very powerful way to think about the education decision of Indigenous peoples, and one that has many years of empirical support. In essence, it makes it explicit that a person will invest in a particular form of education if the benefits of doing so outweigh the costs. That is not to say that people walk around making cost–benefit calculations, estimating future income streams conditional on each individual decision and weighing those up against all other potential investments. There is uncertainty, there is estimation (guesstimation) and there are mental shortcuts that people make. But, the overwhelming evidence suggests that if you live in an area, or you have a particular background for which the benefits of education are larger, or the costs are smaller, you are more likely to see that as being worthwhile and make the decision to participate (Biddle 2013).

Where the HCM becomes useful for understanding Indigenous marginalisation is when you expand the model to take into account the social costs and benefits of education, as well as the different preferences that many Indigenous peoples have articulated for decades, if not centuries. These preferences aren't always or even usually in exclusion to mainstream notions of development like a stable income, engaging employment, a stable home and a healthy life. But, there are Indigenous-specific goals and aspirations that factor into any cost–benefit analysis, including access to land, maintenance of language and ongoing production of culture.

The data presented in this book has shown that there are economic returns to education for Indigenous peoples. Controlling for education explains a large part of the gap in income/employment between Indigenous and non-Indigenous peoples and, more importantly for applying the HCM, those Indigenous peoples with relatively high levels of education tend to have better employment prospects, higher income, improved health and higher subjective wellbeing. Gaps in outcomes still remain though. So, while education is clearly important, experiences of labour market discrimination, locational disadvantage and other barriers to economic engagement still remain. These require a concerted policy effort.

Understanding these economic returns is important. There is sometimes a narrative that there is no point in an Indigenous person engaging in formal education, as there are no jobs or other negative outcomes are somehow inevitable. The data and evidence presented in this book and elsewhere show that this is far from the case. But this book has also shown that there are social costs to education (including unfair treatment by peers and teachers) and the quality of education that Indigenous people have access to does not always match the quality available to non-Indigenous people.

To put the above in a slightly different way, there are two additional types of capital that can support the generation of human capital among Indigenous peoples: social capital (who you know and the networks that you are able to draw upon) and financial capital (the economic resources that you have available to you to support your study). There is an increasing amount of research that shows the importance of these for the education decision (Coleman 2000) and for the education decision of Indigenous peoples (White, Spence et al. 2005). This book has attempted to incorporate some of this discussion into the Human Capital Model, showing how low levels of social or financial capital can increase the costs of education and reduce the benefits.

There were three main sets of policies that were discussed in this book, and lessons can be gained from all of them. First, with regard to school-based responses, we need to keep in mind that often the most effective target of policies to improve the human capital of Indigenous peoples is not the Indigenous population itself, but the broader population. In *Narragunnawali,* this was teachers and early childhood educators, but also non-Indigenous school mates. The former are those that are likely to make the difference between an Indigenous youth in school feeling that they are treated fairly or not. The latter (non-Indigenous students) will be the workmates, subordinates, bosses, police officers, shop owners, etc. that will in future impact on the returns to the education investments that Indigenous peoples are now making.

A second set of policies relates to Indigenous-specific schools and institutions. Historically, these institutions have been run by non-Indigenous administrators and for the purposes of assimilation. They have not surprisingly been shown to have very negative effects on Indigenous maintenance of language and culture, albeit with some evidence that they have positioned some Indigenous peoples favourably within the economic structure of non-Indigenous society. More recent types of institutions (for example Māori boarding schools or Tribal Universities and Colleges in North America) have strong potential to support the economic returns that formal education brings, while minimising some of the social costs experienced by Indigenous peoples.

The final set of policy responses discussed relates to income support for the family and household. An Indigenous child or youth cannot engage with formal education (Indigenous-specific or otherwise) if they are experiencing financial hardship, residential instability, or other forms of financial stress. Despite claims to the contrary, there is no evidence that cash transfers to families reduce engagement with the labour market. While there is mixed evidence on whether cash transfers need to be conditional or not, there is strong evidence that punitive approaches have far more costs than they do benefits. That is, if conditionality is required, then make the transfers a condition of positive investments, rather than make welfare payments at risk from negative behaviour.

We have a good idea in Indigenous education policy about what tends to work in general, and some idea on what would appear to be less effective (including the above). For example, we know from Australian and overseas experience that those who have been exposed to high quality early childhood education have better outcomes than those who haven't. We know that there is a non-linear relationship with class size, with very large classes being detrimental, but very small classes not having high returns.

But the devil is almost always in the detail. What has been shown to work in one country may not work within Australia, or for particular population groups in Australia. For example, conditional cash transfers have been shown to work in a number of developing countries, but have been less effective in developed countries (see Miller, Riccio et al. (2015) for an evaluation of a large-scale trial in New York City). We don't know, therefore, whether they would work for Indigenous children in more developed parts of the world.

The reason why we don't know as much as we should within the field of education on what policies and programmes are effective and which are not, is that we haven't invested in the type of rigorous trial and error approach that is routine in other domains. Nor have we made use of the extensive administrative datasets to anywhere near their full capacity.

Many empirical research questions related to education are concerned principally with correlations. We may be interested in the geographic distribution of students from a low-income or Indigenous background, under the assumption that these students require a greater level of educational support. There are other research and policy questions, however, that are explicitly concerned with causality. Did a particular policy or does a particular behaviour directly affect a particular outcome? For these questions, observational data is less useful.

We can try to answer such questions by comparing the outcomes *ex post* of those individuals who were in one group (for example those who participated in a programme) with those who were in a different group (those who didn't participate). Often, we can use longitudinal data to look at the change in outcomes across the different groups. These comparisons are useful, but we cannot be sure whether the differences in outcomes are driven by the programme itself (a causal effect), whether the outcomes affected participation (reverse causality), or whether there is a third variable or set of variables that affect both (unobserved heterogeneity).

We can try to recover this causal inference using econometric techniques (controlling for observable characteristics), theory/logic, baseline data or some other information about the programme. However, such arguments and techniques are always going to be open to criticism or counter-claim. Perhaps there is some crucial characteristic that cannot be controlled for. Perhaps there is an alternative theory that suggests a different causal pathway. Even with baseline or longitudinal data, something else may have happened that affects outcomes between the two observation periods. The fundamental evaluation problem remains – we can't observe the same individual in two different states. Without careful design, we don't have a counterfactual.

The only way to overcome the evaluation problem is to make sure the two groups being compared are exactly the same at the base period, based on both observable and unobservable characteristics. That is, we set up our comparison groups *ex ante* rather than *ex post*. Or, following Torgerson and Torgerson (2008):

> We assemble a population for whom intervention is appropriate ...; we then allocate the participants to two or more groups and apply the intervention(s) to the groups formed by randomisation; at some pre-specified time in the future we measure the groups in

terms of their outcomes – if there is differences between the groups, and assuming that the difference and the sample size are sufficient, we can infer a causal relationship between our intervention and the group differences.

Within education policy internationally, the number of rigorous randomised trials has reached a significant enough level that Fryer (2017) was able to publish a review article of the results and implications of randomised field experiments in the areas of early childhood education, home-based interventions and school education. The author defined a field experiment as 'any intervention that uses a *verifiably* random procedure to assign participants to treatment and control groups in a non-laboratory environment.' Fryer Jr and colleagues were able to generate usable results from 196 of these in developed countries. From this review, the author was able to conclude that:

> Early childhood investments, on average, significantly increase achievement. Yet, experiments that attempt to alter the home environment in which children are reared in have shown very little success at increasing student achievement. Among school experiments, high-dosage tutoring and 'managed' professional development for teachers have shown to be effective. Ironically, high-dosage tutoring of adolescents seems to be as effective – if not more effective – than early childhood investments. This argues against the growing view that there is a point at which investments in youth are unlikely to yield significant returns ... Lastly, charter schools can be effective avenues of achievement-increasing reform, though the evidence on other market-based approaches such as vouchers or school choice have less demonstrated success.

While highlighting the increase in trials (and evidence) in recent years, Fryer (2017) was also able to conclude that:

> In the 1960s we saw the Perry preschool experiment and the income maintenance experiments, in the 1970s the Abecedarian project was initiated, and in the 1980s there was Project STAR, the Tennessee class size experiment. The data from these randomized experiments alone were used for decades to investigate many interesting questions about how to best produce human capital.

However, he also made clear that the number of trials has increased exponentially (in his words), pointing out that:

In 2000, 14 percent of reviewed education publications on What Works Clearinghouse met their standards without reservations, a distinction given only to well-designed studies that have comparison groups determined through a random process. By 2010, that number had tripled to over 46 percent.

The same could not be said for trials that focus on Indigenous populations. As far as I was able to tell, not a single one of the trials reported in Fryer (2017) had a focus on Indigenous peoples. When Harrison, Goldfeld et al. (2012) wrote an article for the Australian Institute of Health and Welfare's Closing the Gap Clearinghouse (focused on what works within Indigenous policy), one of their main conclusions was that 'There have been no rigorous trials or evaluations of early childhood programmes in Australia, particularly programmes for Indigenous and at-risk children.' While this was several years ago, it is fair to say that this situation hasn't changed much in the intervening years.

That is not to say that there aren't lessons from such review articles, even if they don't focus on Indigenous-specific programmes. The general lessons are that 'Experiments in early childhood education and schools can be particularly effective at producing human capital' but that 'Interventions that attempt to lower poverty, change neighbourhoods, or otherwise alter the home environment in which children are reared have produced surprisingly consistent and precisely estimated "zero" results.'

Of course, the vast majority of Indigenous peoples live in developing countries, where the circumstances and decision-making context is very different from the trials summarised by Fryer (2017). In a related piece in the same volume, Muralidharan (2017) summarised the evidence from a very large number of trials in a developing country context. His summary is worth repeating in detail:

'business-as-usual' expansion of spending on school inputs (which is where the majority of education spending is allocated) may have only modest impacts on improving education outcomes. The main reason for this appears to be that the binding constraints to better performance of developing country education systems many not be inputs but rather: (1) outdated pedagogy that focuses on completing textbooks without accounting for the fact that millions of new first-generation learners may be considerably behind the levels assumed by the textbook; a problem that gets worse in older grades; and (2) weak governance with poor accountability for teachers and other front-line service providers. Thus, these appear to be the most important areas to focus attention on, in addition to designing effective demand-side interventions.

These findings have resonance for the application of the HCM to Indigenous development that I have been discussing throughout this book. The following areas of intervention have been shown to be effective in field trials: looking at the individual barriers that stop students seeing the benefits of education outweighing the costs (and ensuring they actually do); designing a curriculum that is relevant to Indigenous students; and targeting the approach that teachers take to teaching and the way they treat their students. These interventions would be supported by a broader set of Indigenous-specific evidence.

While clearly very powerful, the randomised controlled trials (RCTs) of the type used in Fryer (2017) and Muralidharan (2017) cannot simply be replicated in the context of understanding Indigenous human capital development. Research on Indigenous education has tended to be qualitative. While important for a rich description, Walter and Andersen (2013) make it clear that this need not be the case. But, there are principles of ethical research related to Indigenous peoples, in terms of consent, community ownership and ensuring that the findings are of benefit to Indigenous peoples (though that should not mean not reporting negative findings). These would need to be incorporated into any RCTs that attempt to test ways to improve the human capital development of Indigenous peoples. But, if policy makers and community leaders want to know if something works to achieve those aims (and stop those programmes that don't), then there is no substitute for a large, representative sample of participants, alongside a properly constructed and otherwise identical counterfactual group.

Ultimately, education equity, where Indigenous peoples have the same level of access and positive engagement with education as non-Indigenous peoples, is integral to all other policy aims for Indigenous peoples. Education equity is not going to be achieved, however, unless policy makers think carefully about what the barriers to education are and why so many Indigenous people don't see the benefits of education as outweighing the costs. These benefits and costs are made more clear when we take into account the importance to Indigenous peoples of the maintenance of traditional knowledge, land, language and culture; diversity in Indigenous aspirations; and the importance of an Indigenous voice in designing education policy.

References

Adnett, N. and P. Davies (2002). "Education as a positional good: implications for market-based reforms of state schooling." *British Journal of Educational Studies* **50**(2): 189–205.

Biddle, N. (2013). "Necessary but not sufficient? Youth responses to localised returns to education in Australia." *Education Economics* **21**(1): 92–104.

Coleman, J. S. (2000). "Social capital in the creation of human capital." In E. L. Lesser (ed.), *Knowledge and social capital*, Elsevier: 17–41.

Fryer, R. G. (2017). "The Production of Human Capital in Developed Countries: Evidence from 196 Randomized Field Experiments." *Handbook of Economic Field Experiments* **2**: 95–322.

Harrison, L., S. Goldfeld, E. Metcalfe and T. Moore (2012). *Early learning programs that promote children's developmental and educational outcomes*, AIHW.

Hollis, M. (1982). "Education as a positional good." *Journal of Philosophy of Education* **16**(2): 235–244.

Miller, C., J. Riccio, N. Verma, S. Nuñez, N. Dechausay and E. Yang (2015). "Testing a conditional cash transfer program in the US: the effects of the family rewards program in New York City." *IZA Journal of Labor Policy* **4**(1): 1–29.

Muralidharan, K. (2017). "Field experiments in education in developing countries." In E. Duflo and A. Banerjee (eds), *Handbook of Economic Field Experiments*, Elsevier. **2**: 323–385.

Torgerson, D. J. and C. Torgerson (2008). *Designing randomised trials in health, education and the social sciences: an introduction*, New York: Palgrave Macmillan.

Van de Werfhorst, H. G. (2011). "Skills, positional good or social closure? The role of education across structural–institutional labour market settings." *Journal of Education and Work* **24**(5): 521–548.

Walter, M. and C. Andersen (2013). *Indigenous statistics: A quantitative research methodology*, New York: Left Coast Press.

White, J., N. Spence and P. Maxim (2005). "Social capital and educational attainment among Aboriginal peoples: Canada, Australia and New Zealand." *Policy Research Initiative Social Capital Project Series, Social Capital in Action: Thematic Studies*: 66–81.

Index

Printed in the United States
by Baker & Taylor Publisher Services